The Freedom Wars:

Freedom and Prosperity in
The Possibilities Economy

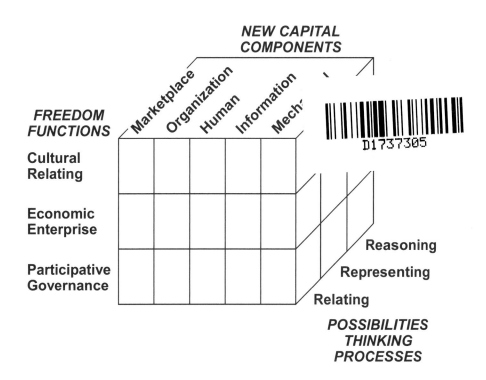

Robert R. Carkhuff, Ph.D., Bernard G. Berenson, Ph.D., Andrew H. Griffin, D.Ed.,
with
John T. Kelly, D.Sci., Rob Owen, M.B.A., Hernan Oyarzabal, D.Sci.,
Debbie D. Anderson, D.Ed., Robert W. Carkhuff, B.A. and Don Collins, M.B.A.

Copyright © 2004, Possibilities Publishing, Inc.

Published by: Possibilities Publishing
22 Amherst Road
Amherst, MA 01002
800-822-2801 (U.S. and Canada)
413-253-3488
413-253-3490 (fax)
Carkhuff.com
HRDPress.com
FreedomDoctrine.org

Editorial services by Don Benoit
Production services by Jean Miller
Cover design by Eileen Klockars

Printed in Canada

THE FREEDOM WARS:

FREEDOM AND PROSPERITY IN THE POSSIBILITIES ECONOMY

Contents

"I have sworn upon the alter of God
eternal hostility over every form of tyranny
over the mind of man."

– Thomas Jefferson

ABOUT THE AUTHORS

ROBERT R. CARKHUFF, PH.D., is Founder and Chairman, **The Carkhuff Group of Corporations,** and CEO, **Freedom Doctrine International.** One of the most-cited scientists of the 20th century, he is author of *The New Science of Possibilities, The Freedom Doctrine* and *The Possibilities Economy.*

BERNARD G. BERENSON, PH.D., is Executive Director, **Carkhuff Institute of Applied Science** and Chairman, **The Freedom Doctrine International.** Co-Founder and Director of the first **Center for Human Resource Development, American International College,** he is author of *The Possibilities Mind* and *The Philosophy of Possibilities Science.*

ANDREW H. GRIFFIN, D.ED., is Assistant Superintendent of Schools, **Washington State,** and author of **"The Possibilities Community"** in *The Freedom Doctrine* as well as co-author of *Freedom-Building.*

DEBBIE D. ANDERSON, D.ED., is Director, Graduate Training in Human Resource Development, **American International College,** and author of **"The Possibilities Humans"** in *The Freedom Doctrine.*

ROBERT W. CARKHUFF, B.A., is Chief Executive Officer, **Human Resource Development Press, Inc.,** and a contributing author to *Freedom-Building.*

DON COLLINS, M.B.A., is Chief Information Officer, **Human Resource Development Press, Inc.,** and a contributor to the statistical analysis and representation of this work.

JOHN T. KELLY, D.SCI., is Director Emeritus, Advanced Systems Design, **IBM, Inc.** and co-author, *The Possibilities Economy* and *The GICCA Curve—The Possibilities Marketplace.*

ROB OWEN, M.B.A., is President, **Freedom Doctrine International** and President of **F³ International,** and a contributing author to *The Freedom Doctrine.*

HERNAN OYARZABAL, D.SCI., former Executive Director, **International Monetary Fund,** is Vice President, **Freedom Doctrine International** and a contributing author to *Freedom-Building.*

Dedicated to:

James Drasgow, Ph.D., who devoted his enormous intellect and life's energies to guiding us in pursuit of **The Freedom Doctrine.**

PREFACE

Freedom Versus Totalitarianism

The most critical battles of civilization lie before us: **Freedom Versus Totalitarianism. Freedom** is dedicated to empowering and releasing all potential—human and otherwise. **Totalitarianism** is dedicated to imposing itself and restraining human behavior.

Freedom enables us to actualize our own changeable destinies. **Totalitarianism** is dedicated only to the perpetuation of its own tautological prowess.

Today, the battles occur not only in the nations of the East but in communities, cultures and countries around the world. Indeed, we see video images of the mad scramble of South American *"leaders"* to participate in *"photo ops"* with Castro, the symbol of **Totalitarianism.**

The battles are heard not only in the language of *"men"* in the East who reject participative governance in favor of theocratic dictatorships, but also in the commands of *"bosses"* in the West who retard the mechanisms of economics, as well as educators who impose standards of learning from another era.

What is it that the **Totalitarian** ideologies have to offer? Nothing at all, outside of the echoes of a holocaustic 20th century that exterminated 150 million people.

What is it that the **Freedom** ideologies have to offer? Everything—and more than we can now conceive!

The **Freedom Wars** are the most important battles of our time—or, indeed, any time. They establish that **Freedom** and **Prosperity** are directly and powerfully related. As we move up in **Freedom,** we move up in **Prosperity** and its correlates, **Peace** and **Participation.**

In this book you will find an introduction to the models and tools needed to help anyone and everyone win **The Freedom Wars.**

RRC, BGB and AHG   June 2004
McLean, VA

FOREWORD
Eclipsing All Great Works

Thomas Jefferson dedicated his life's mission to the freedom of our minds. This mission is at risk.

Today, many people around the world are willing to surrender their freedoms for the apparency of security, especially economic security. So have we failed in our war for freedom?

For scientists, freedom is found in our repertoires of responses: the more responses, the greater freedom. Indeed, without the responses, we cannot even discriminate the opportunity for their free expression or application.

For the possibilities scientists, freedom is a function of our thinking or processing responses; again, the more thinking, the greater freedom. Indeed, with these processing responses we can generate our own degrees of freedom.

Essentially, then, freedom is found in our ability to generate new and more productive responses to the changing conditions of our times. To be sure, true freedom is found in our ability to generate the changes in the conditions of our times.

Just as we create free individuals by empowering them in thinking responses, so do we create free organizations, communities, cultures, nations and marketplaces by empowering them with appropriate processing responses.

For cultures and nations and markets, these processing responses have to do with the development of freedom's resources:

- **Socially**-empowered processing that enables **interdependent cultural relating;**

- **Economically**-empowered processing that enables **entrepreneurial free enterprise;**

- **Politically**-empowered processing that enables **direct participative governance.**

Together, these conditions define **The Freedom Functions: interdependent cultural relating, entrepreneurial free enterprise, direct participative governance.**

Jefferson did have it right! The wars are between freedom and tyranny. The battles are for our minds. Our resources are in our thinking skills.

In this context, **"The Freedom Wars"** is a crowning achievement of civilization. It orients us to infinite possibilities to generate fresh, new and elevating ideas and events. Humankind may now reach beyond its past conditioning to become free and generative, elevating and evolving, interdependent forces of Nature.

James Drasgow, Ph.D.,
Professor Emeritus,
S.U.N.Y., Buffalo

I. THE FREEDOM WARS

1. Freedom and Prosperity

THE FREEDOM FUNCTIONS

Stages of Freedom-Building	Cultural Relating	Economic Enterprise	Participative Governance	Stages of Civilization
Leader	Free Interdependent	Free Enterprise	Free Democratic	21st Century
Contributor	Collaborative	Capitalistic	Representative	Late 20th Century
Participant	Independent	Mixed	Mixed	Mid 20th Century
Observer	Competitive	Command	Authoritarian	Early 20th Century
Detractor	Dependent	Control	Totalitarian	Pre-20th Century

GROWTH ↑

SURVIVAL

People such as Webster like to define freedom in the negative: **"The exemption from slavery, servitude, confinement, or constraint."** Modern Americans, in particular, think of *"The Underground Railway"* of Pre-Civil War as the defining moment of freedom: runaway slaves following *"The Freedom Road"* north.

But what if the blacks came to a crossroads on a cloudy night when they had no stars or instructions to guide them? Were they free to choose? Moreover, were they free to make enlightened and freeing choices? These are the essential questions of freedom:

1. **Are we free to choose?**
2. **Can we choose in an enlightened manner?**

No choices are as profound as those made by the runaway slaves! Yet we must ask: *Were they free choices?*

At another level, Robert Frost, the great American Poet, has written free-style poetry which has placed before all of us the question of free choice:

> *"Two roads diverged in the woods,*
> *And I, I took the one less-traveled by*
> *And that has made all the difference."*

In so writing, Frost has assumed that there are a finite number of choices before us and that we must choose between them.

In fact, there are an infinite number of possible choices and we must learn to generate them. The only real freedom is in our repertoire of responses for processing or thinking. For God has given us **Human Brainpower** with an infinite capacity for generating new responses. All we need to do is to learn the guiding principles for exercising freedom.

Freedom for Nations

Freedom is the exercise of choice in the face of definable conditions. We have chosen to define freedom for individuals in terms of the repertoire of processing responses. The same definitions hold under differing conditions for organizations, communities, cultures, markets and, yes, nations. All define freedom by their ability to process the conditions of their existence, often in the moment, always in the crisis. Freedom may be defined operationally by **The Freedom Matrix** (See Figure 1). This is a two-dimensional matrix comprised of interacting scales for values and requirements.

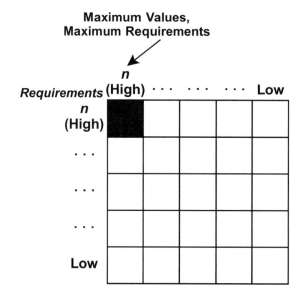

Figure 1. The Freedom Matrix

To better understand **The Freedom Matrix,** individuals may think of themselves going for a job interview:

- **Values** are the things that people would like to acquire by attaining the job—things like pay, location, comfort, security and fulfillment (Values 1 through n).

- **Requirements** are the things that the job wants from the people they hire—things like showing up, having skills, performing tasks, being productive and maybe even profitable (Requirements 1 through n).

In effect, the job's values become the individual's requirements. Similarly, the individual's values become the job's requirements: recruiters position the jobs to be attractive to people who are attractive to them.

It is similar for all other levels of conditions. **All entities relate values and requirements in healthy attempts to maximize meeting both at the highest levels.**

Nations seeking to join the **Global Village** or enter the **Global Marketplace** have similar choices. They have values for joining: participation, peace, prosperity. In turn, the market presents requirements for being chosen: participation, peace, prosperity! In this instance, the values and requirements focus upon the same dimensions. The differences may be found in the standards of **The Freedom Functions.**

In this context, then, we define **Freedom** as a function of the following:

> *The extraordinary quantity and quality of processing systems of all kinds, dedicated to elevating the rational principles of a continuously-changing civilization.*

In turn, we define **Totalitarianism** as a function of the following:

> *The surrender of processing potential to the will of the necessarily-limited "master" who promises the illusion of stability and the delusion of competence.*

Again, **Freedom** is **Processing:** a function of our repertoire of generative responses to changing stimuli. **Totalitarianism** is **Conditioning:** a function of our conditioned responses to unchanging stimuli.

The Freedom Functions

The Freedom Functions define the **Freedom Architecture** for the standards of **Freedom** for all nations. They emphasize the levels of freedom that nations must achieve in order to meet the requirements for participation, contribution and leadership in the **Global Village and its Marketplace** (See Table 1).

Table 1. The Freedom Architecture

THE FREEDOM FUNCTIONS

	Stages of Freedom-Building	Cultural Relating	Economic Enterprise	Participative Governance	Stages of Civilization
GROWTH	Leader	Free Interdependent	Free Enterprise	Free Democratic	21st Century
	Contributor	Collaborative	Capitalistic	Representative	Late 20th Century
	Participant	Independent	Mixed	Mixed	Mid 20th Century
	Observer	Competitive	Command	Authoritarian	Early 20th Century
	Detractor	Dependent	Control	Totalitarian	Pre-20th Century
SURVIVAL					

As may be noted, **The Freedom Functions** define the dimensions of **Freedom for Nations:**

- **Cultural Relating** or the degrees of relatedness within, between and among cultures and nations;

- **Free Enterprise** or the degrees of freedom in economic enterprise within, between and among cultures and nations;

- **Participative Governance** or the degrees of participation in governance within, between and among cultures and nations.

Together, **The Freedom Functions** define **The Freedom Architecture** for entry and elevation in **The 21st Century Global Marketplace.**

Cultural Relating

With constructive relating, all human endeavors are probable with a 95% degree of certitude. With constructive **Cultural Relating** at high levels, all national initiatives are possible with a similarly high degree of certainty. The plain fact of the matter is that nations cannot trade if they do not relate. Emphatically, nations cannot trade in **The Global Marketplace** without relating in **The Cultural Marketplace!**

In this context, the levels of **Cultural Relating** are defined in **The Freedom Model:***

Level 5:	**Free and interdependent relating** is defined by **"mutual processing for mutual benefit"** with other cultures and/or nations.
Level 4:	**Collaborative relating** is defined by shared goals and common means to achieve the goals with other cultures and/or nations.
Level 3:	**Independent relating** is defined by reserving the right and power to compete as well as cooperate with other cultures and/or nations.
Level 2:	**Competitive relating** is defined by achieving and maintaining the *"competitive edge"* with other cultures and nations.
Level 1:	**Dependent relating** is defined by dependency in relating with other cultures and nations, including adapting and reacting.

These definitions will be enriched in the **Cultural Relating** applications that follow.

---

* These definitions are elaborated upon in R. R. Carkhuff, et al, **The Freedom Doctrine,** HRD Press, 2003.

Economic Enterprise

The key to the highest levels of **Economic Enterprise** is the modifier, **"Free".** It is not the trade that defines it. It is the free thinking that generates initiatives to meet consumer needs that defines it. Specialty products make trade attractive. Trade agreements without attractive products are like rental properties without occupants. The plain fact of the matter is that nations cannot trade if they do not have something of value. And they will not have something of value if they cannot generate substance!

In this context, the levels of **Economic Enterprise** are defined in **The Freedom Model:**

Level 5:   **Free and interdependent enterprise economics** defined by **"mutual trading for mutual benefit"** with other nations;

Level 4:   **Capitalistic economics** defined by maximizing financial capital-based investments and minimizing governmental burdens;

Level 3:   **Mixed economics** defined by occasional or intermittently capitalistic and command practices;

Level 2:   **Command economics** defined by intentional governmental command practices;

Level 1:   **Control economics** defined by total governmental control of economic practices.

Again, these definitions will be enriched in the **Free Enterprise** applications that follow.

Participative Governance

In the enlightened, modern world, governance is defined by participation. Government without participation restricts decision-making to a council or a person of increasingly isolated, **Totalitarian** *"mind-sets"*: they or he make decisions about citizens **for** citizens. And with the acceleration of change, they *"know"* increasingly less and less, until they *"know"* nothing about anything! Even when they are over-thrown or replaced, one limited set of variability is replaced by another limited set of variability. The only real discrimination in governance is the degree of participation.

In this context, the levels of **Participative Governance** are defined in **The Freedom Model:**

Level 5: **Free and interdependent democratic governance** defined by direct and **"mutually beneficial"** relations between citizens and decision-makers;

Level 4: **Representative democratic governance** defined by citizen relations with representatives who represent them with decision-makers;

Level 3: **Mixed governance** as defined by occasional or intermittent democratic and authoritarian activities;

Level 2: **Authoritarian governance** as defined by intentional governmental edicts;

Level 1: **Totalitarian governance** as defined by total control of political practices.

Again, these definitions will be enriched in the **Participative Governance** applications that follow.

The Freedom Outcomes

It is widely believed that any indices of **Freedom** are related to everything that is good in the world: participation, intelligence, creativity, performance, and, yes, peace. However, the evidence from research is limited. Moreover, the research does not specify the programs and objectives for elevating **Freedom** in operational terms.

An exception to these beliefs has been the work of The Heritage Foundation which has been the forerunner in assessing the effects of **Economic Freedom.** Defining **Economic Freedom** as *"the absence of government coercion"* upon the private sector, the researchers accounted for much of the variance in **Prosperity** through the following measures: trade policy, fiscal burdens, government intervention, monetary policy, capital flows, banking and finance, wages and prices, property rights, regulation and black market.

In our own work, we have studied the relationship between **Prosperity** and **The Freedom Functions: Cultural Relating, Economic Enterprise, Participative Government.** In Figure 2, we present the relationship of our **Freedom Scores** and **Prosperity** measured in **Per Capita Gross Domestic Product** or **GDP.**

As may be noted, in the **"Power Curve"** there is a high relationship between **Freedom** and **Per Capita GDP: high scores on The Freedom Functions earn high GDP and vice versa.** This means that, as the **Freedom Index** moves toward **"Free,"** the **Per Capita GDP** moves upward many thousands of dollars. Conversely, as the nations move toward **"Detractor,"** the **Per Capita Indices** move toward low earnings, ultimately numbered in hundreds of dollars per year.

The correlation between **Freedom Scores** and **Prosperity Indices** is high. Depending upon the measures, approximately three-quarters of the variability in **Prosperity Indices** is accounted for by the variance of **Freedom Scores.**

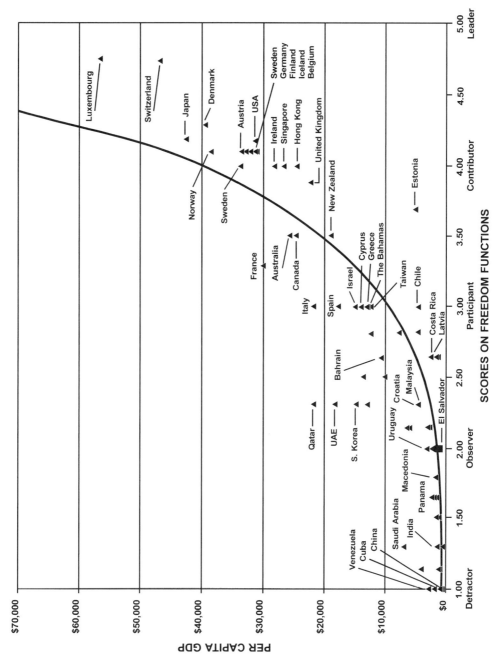

Figure 2. Freedom and Prosperity

The correlation is not a perfect one-to-one correspondence: one movement up in earnings for one movement over in **Freedom.** That is because of other factors; for example, some nations that are totalitarian may be also rich in resources such as energy—so they get **"middling earnings."**

In this context, the figure presents the images of **"The Past, The Present and The Future of Civilization:"**

- The **"Past"** is found in the clustered low scores on **The Freedom Functions** of **"The Detractors"** who live in a version of **"The Pre-20th Century Civilization:"**

  - **Dependent Cultural Relating,**
  - **Controlling Economic Enterprise,**
  - **Totalitarian Governance.**

- The **"Transition from The Past to The Present"** is discovered in the **"Middling scores"** of **"The Observers"** who live in a version of **"The Early 20th Century Civilization:"**

  - **Competitive Cultural Relating,**
  - **Command Economics,**
  - **Authoritarian Governance.**

- The **"Present"** is represented in the mixed scores of **"The Participants"** who have only begun to embrace **Freedom** in a version of **"The Mid-20th Century Civilization:"**

  - **Independent Cultural Relating;**
  - **Mixed Enterprise Economics,**
  - **Mixed Governance.**

- The **"Transition to The Future"** is found in the high scores of **"The Contributors"** who are committed to becoming **Free and Prosperous** in a version of **"The Late 20th Century Civilization:"**

- • **Collaborative Cultural Relating,**
- • **Capitalistic Enterprise Economics,**
- • **Representative Democratic Governance.**

- • The **"Future"** is modeled in the exemplary performance of **"The Leaders"** who are attempting to commit fully to becoming **Free and Prosperous in "The 21st Century Civilization:"**

  - • **Interdependent Cultural Relating,**
  - • **Free Enterprise Economics,**
  - • **Direct Democratic Governance.**

Indeed, all peoples of all nations may become **Free and Prosperous. The Freedom Architecture** is modeled by **The Exemplary Performers** on **The Freedom Functions.** This is the foundation for all **Possibilities Civilization.**

To be sure, **there are no prosperous Totalitarian Nations!**

Only nations striving toward **Freedom** receive the **Rewards of Freedom.**

The **Threshold for Prosperity** appears to be at **The Participant Level of the Freedom Functions** (Level 3.0):

- • Peoples and nations that relate with **Cultural Independence,** meaning **Collaborative** or **Competitive** according to the conditions and their requirements;

- • Peoples and nations that engage in **Mixed Enterprise Economics,** meaning **Capitalistic** or by **Command** as appropriate to their conditions;

- • Peoples and nations that engage in **Mixed Governance,** meaning **Representative** or **Authoritarian** according to their circumstances.

At **The Participant Level,** then, nations range in the $10,000–$20,000 **Per Capita GDP.**

Above **The Participant Level,** nations and peoples take off in growing and, then, spiraling levels of **Prosperity.** At **The Contributor Level** (above Level 4.0), the modal earnings are in the range of $30,000 **Per Capita GDP.** Approaching **The Leader Level** (above Level 4.5), a nation such as Switzerland earns above $45,000 while Luxembourg reaches over $56,000 **Per Capita GDP.**

Below **The Participant Level,** nations are poor. At **The Observer Level** (above Level 2.0), where nations have not yet committed themselves to **Freedom,** the **Per Capita GDP** ranges below $5,000. At **The Detractor Level** where many of the nations are reactive and even destructive, the earnings range in the hundreds of dollars.

This, indeed, may be the most important correlational figure of our time—or any time! **Freedom is directly and powerfully related to generating Prosperity and all of its related values—peace and participation!**

In summary, **we reap what we sow!** Put another way, we get what we **process** for. If we process for **Freedom in Collaborative Cultural Relating, Free Enterprise Economics** and **Participative Democratic Governance,** we will achieve untold **Possibilities of Prosperity** and **Enlightenment.**

If, on the other hand, we plan for **Control in Totalitarian Governance and Command Economics,** we will achieve the unreported problems of isolation, poverty and ignorance.

In transition, **Freedom** assumes the **Infinite Potential of Human Brainpower** and empowers us to generate, not only a continuously-expanding economy but also **Our Continuously-Changing Destiny.** Its adherents learn more and more about more and more until they know a great deal about an **Evolving-Everything.**

Totalitarianism assumes the finite nature of all resources from which derives both an **Economy of Scarcity, a Psychology of Stasis** and a **Pathology of Discrimination.** Its practitioners know less and less about less and less until, finally, they know nothing about anything.

On a lighter note, **The Great Baseball Philosopher,** Yogi Berra, is credited with making the following statement on **Freedom of Choice:**

"When you come to the fork in the road, take it!"

In a very real sense, that is the story of **Freedom:** that we—nations as well as individuals—have the capacity to make any and all choices; that we can be empowered to understand the implications of these choices; and that we can act upon these choices and, with feedback, improve the choices.

In short, **Freedom** is a function of our capacities to generate new choices. So when you come to the fork in the road, **take the fork! Please, take the fork!**

2. The Freedom Model

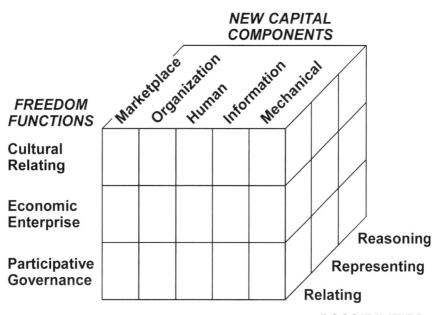

So how do nations establish desired levels of **Freedom?** Like people and organizations, they must have a process for accomplishing high levels of **The Freedom Functions.** For nations, there is such a process. It is labeled **The Freedom Model.**

To this day, there have been no models for progression to **The Freedom Functions** for a variety of reasons. The first and most important reason is that nations do not view themselves in terms of growth models. Prior to entry into the 21st century and **The Global Marketplace,** there have been no reasons to do so. However, just as jobs impose requirements upon their applicants, so does trade generate requirements for our entry into the market: one's trading partners' values become a nation's requirements for participation.

Another reason for the absence of growth models has been that the applications have been limited to the private sector (none in the public sector). One application that has been revealed in sharp relief has been **"The Air Wars"** or **"The NCD Wars"** between Boeing and Airbus, the world's leading aircraft producers. Carkhuff and his associates have submitted an *"x-ray"* vision of the corporate models employed.

The NCD Wars

Boeing, the historical market leader, relied upon *"legacy-driven,"* marketplace positioning. Confident in their market dominance, Boeing executives emphasized the policy of *"the front runner:"* customizing the standard versions of proven aircrafts so as to minimize their risks and maximize their profits.

Airbus, in turn, had the psychology of *"second place"* and *"trying harder"* along with high fear of failure. Insecure in their lack of competitiveness, their executives instituted **New Capital Development:**[*]

---

[*] R. R. Carkhuff, et al, *The Possibilities Economy,* HRD Press, 2004.

- Positioning interdependently to create **Marketplace Capital;**
- Aligning interdependently to develop **Organizational Capital;**
- Processing interdependently to generate **Human Capital;**
- Modeling interdependently to establish **Information Capital;**
- Tooling interdependently to produce **Mechanical Capital.**

These are the ingredients of **New Capital Development** or **NCD.** Together, these ingredients organize the systems to generate **NCD** in the implementation of marketplace positioning.

The marketplace positioning that Airbus assumed was to engage all parties in the production of their aircraft: potential competitors as well as customers, vendors as well as suppliers, representatives of the community as well as the corporation.

Utilizing electronic **Computer-Assisted Design** or **CAD Systems,** the positioning that they achieved was pre-potent. Electronically, they were able to tailor virtually infinite designs for aircraft. The operative word is *"virtually."*

In the growth process, Airbus evolved rapidly through the following stages of design:

- **EPD** or **Electronic Product Definition,**
- **IPD** or **Integrated Product Definition,**
- **IP⁵D** or **Integrated Process Development.**

IP⁵D was the culminating stage of process development.

IP⁵D incorporated all of the ingredients of **NCD** as follows:

- **P⁵ – Positioning or Marketplace Capital Development,**
- **P⁴ – Partnering or Organizational Capital Development,**
- **P³ – People or Human Capital Development,**
- **P² – Processing or Information Capital Development,**
- **P¹ – Products or Mechanical Capital Development.**

Together, **IP⁵D** defined the development and the design of ingredients needed for accomplishing **The Freedom Functions.**

The rest, as they say, is history! Airbus' **IP⁵D** policy captured both the imagination of the public and the orders of the customers. At the end of 2003, Airbus culminated **The NCD Wars** by capturing a 55% market-share. Boeing, needless to say, is despondent and desperately attempting to replace substance with political arrangements.

The Think Wars

A second set of wars are relevant to **The Freedom Model.** We label these wars, **"The Think Wars."** Basically, **The Think Wars** are fought over **"Human Brainpower." The Think Wars** begin in pre-school and elementary school and are continued through middle, secondary and post-secondary schooling. They culminate in the workers we employ in business and the citizens we represent in governance.

Succinctly, **The Think Wars** are fought over the levels of empowerment and expectations for human processing or thinking:

- **Conditioned Responding,**
- **Discriminative Learning,**
- **Generative Thinking.**

These three basic models of human processing dictate very different standards.

Conditioned Responding

Conditioned Responding is defined as reflex responses to presentation of stimulus conditions. In effect, no intervention is required between the presentation of stimuli (**S**) and the emittance of the responses (**R**) although there is a phenomenon of **s–r "chaining expectancies"** that bridge the gap (See Figure 3).

Figure 3. Conditioned Responding

Discriminative Learning

Discriminative Learning is defined by the intervention of the human organism between the stimulus and response. The human organism is the repository of **S–R conditioned responding systems.** Basically, the human organism (**O**) discriminates the conditions of the stimuli (**S**) and selects and emits the appropriate responses (**R**) (See Figure 4).

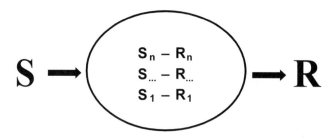

Figure 4. Discriminative Learning

Generative Thinking

Generative Thinking is defined by the intervention of the human processor between the stimulus and the response. The human processor is the repository of **S–O–R Discriminative Learning Systems.** Basically, the human processor (**P**) employs the learning systems to discriminate the stimuli (**S**) and generate or create whole new responses (**R**) that the stimuli were not calculated to elicit (See Figure 5).

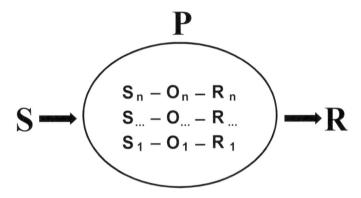

Figure 5. Generative Processing

The Nesting of Processing Systems

The nesting of the processing systems may be viewed in Figure 6. As may be noted, the **S–R Conditioning Systems** have only intervening **"chaining" sequences** while the **S–O–R Learning Systems** incorporate **S–R Conditioning Systems** and the **S–P–R Generating Systems** incorporate **S–O–R Learning Systems.** This means that higher-order processing systems incorporate lower-order processing potential. Indeed, they may later relate the lower-order processing systems exponentially in permutations and combinations.

Clearly, the processing power is in the higher-order **S–P–R Generative Thinking Systems. Generativity** is also the increasingly elevated requirement of **The Global Marketplace**—especially for the leading countries such as America as we will soon discover.

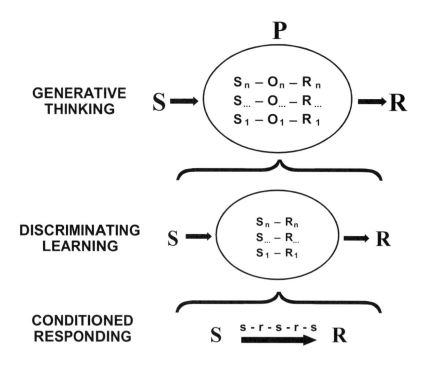

Figure 6. Nested Processing Systems

The Combatants

On the one side of **The Think Wars** are those people who understand that in America today, nearly 80% of the jobs already require thinking skills. These people see the requirements for thinking escalating from **Discriminative Learning Systems** to **Generative Thinking Systems.** This is because the movement of globalization *"farms out"* the jobs requiring **S–R conditioning** to more economical employees with less educated cultures in more attenuated economies. Moreover, increasingly, globalization is also yielding jobs requiring **S–O–R Learning,** including delivering services as well as producing products, to learning cultures and commoditizing economies.

On the other side of **The Think Wars** are those people who lead us retrogressively to the fast-disappearing **S–R** standards of an earlier time. Led by teachers, union leaders and politicians, these **"Luddites"** would have us achieve **"Standards of Learning"** defined in terms of requirements of **The Industrial Age** whose manufacturing jobs have already been **"shipped out."**

Stasis is comforting in virtuality!

Change is generating in reality!

The Change Curriculum

The change curricula is **The Generative Thinking** or **Processing System** or, as we label it, **"The New 3Rs of Thinking."**[*]

We may view the phases of generative processing operations in sharpest relief in the human processing paradigm (See Figure 7). As we may see, the paradigm unfolds as a branching system or tree:

- **R^1 Relating**
  - **Getting images**
  - **Giving images**
  - **Merging images**

- **R^2 Representing**
  - **S^1 Sentences**
  - **S^2 Systems**
  - **S^3 Schematics**

- **R^3 Reasoning**
  - **Exploring** by expanding alternatives,
  - **Understanding** by narrowing to preferred alternatives,
  - **Acting** by doing or by performing tasks to achieve objectives.

Note that *The New 3Rs* are the critical phases in systematically generating new and more powerful responses:

- **Relating** by sharing and merging,
- **Representing** by operationalizing and dimensionalizing,
- **Reasoning** by expanding and narrowing alternatives.

---

[*] R. R. Carkhuff and D. Benoit. *The New 3Rs of Thinking: Possibilities Thinking and Individual Freedom,* HRD Press, 2004.

         2. The Freedom Model

R^1 R^2 R^3 R^3 –   R^3 –   R^3 –
                                EXPANDING   NARROWING   DOING

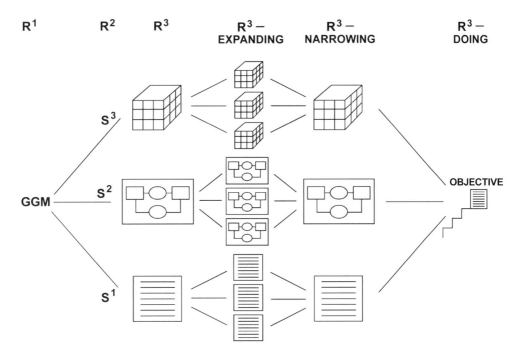

Figure 7. The Generative Processing Paradigm

To sum, working backwards, we cannot do things with creative initiative without expanding and narrowing alternatives: further, we cannot expand and narrow without representing images; finally, we cannot represent images without relating to information. At this point, what is most important is that we understand that generative processing systems do exist.

The Freedom Model

The Freedom Model is comprised of the operational relationships among **The Freedom Functions, The NCD Components,** and **The Generative** or **Possibilities Thinking Processes** (See Figure 8). Operationally, we may say that **The NCD Components** are dedicated to accomplishing **The Freedom Functions.** In so doing, they are enabled by **The Possibilities Thinking Processes.** This means that the **Possibilities Processes** enable the **NCD Components** to accomplish **The Freedom Functions. The Freedom Model** may be employed in representing all efforts to participate in the 21st century **Global Village and Its Marketplace** as we will soon see.

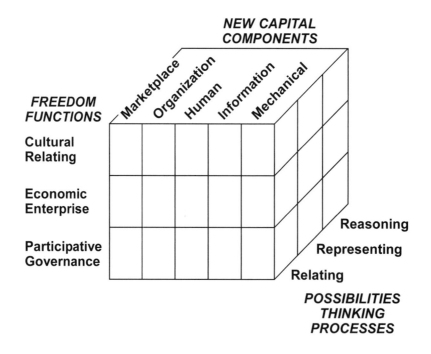

Figure 8. The Freedom Model

The **Freedom Wars** are being fought in all arenas. The wars are being fought between the forces of stasis and change. In the pages that follow, we will illustrate models for accomplishing **Freedom** and correlationally **Prosperity,** peace and participation.

In a lighter vein, with respect to the philosopher, Yogi Berra:

> *When you do not come to a fork in the road, make the forks, folks!*

That is the generativity that the 21st century marketplace requires.

II. THE FREE AND THE UNFREE

3. Singapore — The Global Exemplar

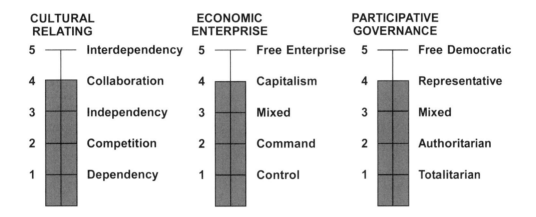

CULTURAL RELATING		ECONOMIC ENTERPRISE		PARTICIPATIVE GOVERNANCE	
5	Interdependency	5	Free Enterprise	5	Free Democratic
4	Collaboration	4	Capitalism	4	Representative
3	Independency	3	Mixed	3	Mixed
2	Competition	2	Command	2	Authoritarian
1	Dependency	1	Control	1	Totalitarian

The tale of the exemplar is the tale of intentionality. Intentionality bridges the gap from the conditions of poverty to the actualization of prosperity. Intentionality is found in the contribution of the leaders of Singapore: intentionality to meet the conditions of **Freedom** in order to realize the largesse of economic **Prosperity.**

Singapore is a small city-state of four million citizens, most of them Chinese with the remainder Malay and Indian. In 1965, Malaysia rejected a union with Singapore, thus leaving Singapore's people to their own strategies for growth. With no real natural resources, Singapore emphasized the intellectual resources of its leaders in generating strategies for socioeconomic growth.

Under the leadership of Lee Kuan Yew, a politician, and Dr. Goh Keng Swee, an economist, Singapore focused upon empowering the system that would generate Singapore's own—and continuously changing—destiny. The leaders began with strategic decisions to join the global village and its marketplace. They continued with images of **"New Capital"** as sources of socioeconomic growth in the **Global Marketplace.** They culminated with educational processes for enabling the **New Capital Development** to accomplish **Global Positioning in the Marketplace.**

The Freedom Functions

The first strategic decision was to join the **Global Village and Its Marketplace.** This decision necessitated addressing the requirements of the 21st century marketplace:

- **Cultural relating with other cultures in the marketplace;**
- **Free enterprise to accomplish economic missions;**
- **Participative governance to empower free enterprise economics.**

Together, these requirements define **The Freedom Functions** of the **21st Century Global Village and Its Marketplace.**

Cultural Relating

In **Cultural Relating,** the Singapore leaders set their goals high (See Figure 9). They committed to transform themselves from dependency to independency in relating. Moreover, they dedicated their intended independency to collaborating with other cultures in the **Global Village.** They were not prepared for interdependent relating at the highest levels for that meant **"mutual processing for mutual benefit"** and they had no fully trustworthy partners. However, they did engage in interdependent processing within Singapore's various agencies in both the public and private sectors.

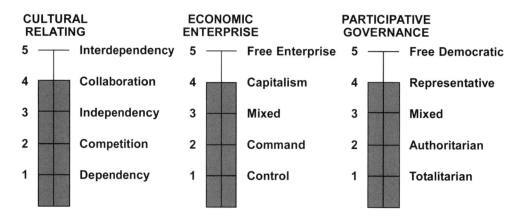

CULTURAL RELATING

5	Interdependency
4	Collaboration
3	Independency
2	Competition
1	Dependency

ECONOMIC ENTERPRISE

5	Free Enterprise
4	Capitalism
3	Mixed
2	Command
1	Control

PARTICIPATIVE GOVERNANCE

5	Free Democratic
4	Representative
3	Mixed
2	Authoritarian
1	Totalitarian

Figure 9. Levels of The Freedom Functions

In short, the Singaporeans are rated at level 4.0 on **Cultural Relating,** reflecting a commitment to collaboration but not yet at the level of the very interdependency that characterized their processing within their own homogenous culture.

Economic Enterprise

The Singaporean leaders were also dedicated to **Free Enterprise** at the highest possible levels (See again Figure 9). In their minds, this meant converting from command and control economies to capitalistic and, ultimately, free enterprise economies. However, their image of **Free Enterprise** was somewhat convoluted. On the one hand, they targeted industries and *"incubated"* GLCs or government-linked companies in preparation for private sector maturity. On the other hand, they envisioned **Free Enterprise** in terms of **Multinational Corporations** with whom they collaborated freely. They did not see the need for the highest level of **Free Enterprise** in **Entrepreneurially-Driven, Free Enterprise Systems.** Accordingly, the Singaporeans are rated level 4.0 on **Free Enterprise:** blessed with a disposition to state-directed entrepreneurial initiatives, they had little understanding of the individualism that, historically, has been the source of generative breakthroughs in the marketplace.

Participative Governance

Once again, within their own limited vision, the Singaporeans were committed to **Participative Democracy** at the highest possible levels (See again Figure 9). In their view, this meant movements from authoritarian and even totalitarian governance to representative democratic governance. While their small city-state encouraged direct interactions on a daily basis, they did not formalize the doctrine of direct democracy upon which a truly global marketplace is predicated: a democracy of direct democracies. Instead, they conceptualized governance—correctly for their purposes—as the support system for empowering state enterprise. However, they did not operationalize governance as the vehicle for empowering and releasing the potentially infinite power of individualism, the prepotent source of entrepreneurial initiative. Accordingly, the Singaporeans are rated level 4.0

on governance with a limited view of individualism as the most powerful source of socioeconomic initiatives.

To sum, the Singaporeans receive ratings of level 4.0 on all of **The Freedom Functions:**

- **Collaborative Relating**
- **Capitalistic Economics**
- **Representative Governance**

The good news is that Singapore is among the highest average ratings of all cultures and countries in the global marketplace. The bad news is that the Singaporean system contains within it the seeds of its own demise: the individual risk-aversion inherent in all national planning systems—witness the exquisitely detailed planning systems of the **Totalitarian Powers** of the 20th century.

The New Capital Components

With the setting of **The Freedom Functions,** the second strategic decision was to define the components or the wherewithal to accomplish the functions. With the growing recognition of the limited nature of **Financial Capital** as the pre-potent source of socioeconomic growth, the Singaporeans addressed other sources of growth:

- **Marketplace positioning in the global village;**
- **Organizational alignment with marketplace positioning;**
- **Human processing to implement the organizational alignment.**

Together, these ingredients define **The New Capital Development** or **NCD Components** dedicated to accomplishing **The Freedom Functions.** We will explore and assess these **NCD** components: marketplace, organization, human.

Marketplace Positioning

The very act of committing to **The Freedom Functions** at level 4.0 had profound implications for marketplace positioning (See Figure 10). Singapore positioned itself in the marketplace as state-sponsored organizations dedicated to accomplishing **The Freedom Functions.** This meant that the state had the capacity to develop the internal and external collaborative organizational alignments needed to accomplish **The Freedom Functions.** It also meant that this focus placed a limit upon its leadership in the marketplace: it could never be a generator of breakthrough technologies; at best, in collaboration with business leaders in the industry it had chosen, it could be an innovator. In any event, their positioning was dedicated to maximizing commercial participation in the marketplace. Accordingly, the Singaporeans rated level 4.0 on innovative positioning in the marketplace: they had the capacity to design and engineer the architecture for their state-sponsored venture capitalism. This meant that they had level 4.0 **MCD** or **Marketplace Capital Development.**

Figure 10. Levels of New Capital Development

Organizational Alignment

The strength of all of Singapore's **NCD** was the organization. Organizational alignment was marketing-driven rather than leadership-driven (See again Figure 10). This meant that marketing drove all other operations: the resource integration to tailor products, services and solutions; the technology development to customize, and the production operations to standardize everything. (Leadership-driven organizations would be initiated by producer organizations to maintain *"comparative advantage"* in meeting customer *needs* rather than *wants* or desires.) Accordingly, the Singaporeans are rated level 4.0 on marketing-driven **OCD** or **Organizational Capital Development** to implement marketplace positioning: responding to customer requirements rather than producer values.

Human Processing

The original resources for all of Singapore's initiatives were leadership resources (See again Figure 10). In this regard, while the human processing that defines leadership capital was goal-driven, it was supplemented by intensive and extensive inputting. The customer and collaborator inputs that implemented the market-driven organizational architecture were the key ingredients in processing and drove all other processes, including planning and outputting. (Goal-driven processing would be initiated by leadership in producer organizations to create the *"competitive edge"* in the marketplace.) Accordingly, the Singaporeans are rated level 4.0 on input-driven **HCD** or **Human Capital Development** to implement organizational alignment with marketplace positioning: marketing-driven organizational alignment to state-entrepreneurial architecture.

To sum, the Singaporeans receive ratings of level 4.0 on all of **The New Capital Development Components** dedicated to achieving **The Freedom Functions:**

- Organizational architecture to define marketplace positioning;

- Marketing-driven organizational alignment to implement marketplace positioning;

- Input-driven human processing to implement organizational alignment.

Again, the good news is that Singapore has the **NCD Components** necessary to accomplish its targeted levels of **The Freedom Functions.** The bad news is that this level of **NCD Components** places a lid on the potential of individual contributors to robust growth in the global marketplace.

The Generative Processes

The third strategic decision was to enable the **NCD Components** to accomplish **The Freedom Functions** by empowering the individuals involved in **Generative Thinking or Processing Systems.** In other words, the leaders committed to teaching their citizens to think initiatively within the system they had defined. The operative words here are *"within the system"* because consensus education places a limit upon the generative processing of individuals.

In this context, we may examine the thinking systems of individuals in the following phases:

- **Relating to phenomena;**
- **Representing phenomena;**
- **Reasoning with phenomena.**

Together, these phases define **Generative Thinking Processes** or **Possibilities Thinking Systems** that we will explore and assess.

Relating Systems

Generative Thinking Processes require **Relating Systems.** However, with the emphasis upon collaborative processing, there are no systems beyond the sharing of images and the developing of consensus (See Figure 11). In other words, there are no systematic ways to relate fully with phenomena, human and otherwise:

- **Getting information by responding accurately to others' images of phenomena;**
- **Giving information by initiating effectively to present one's own images;**
- **Merging information by negotiating personalized images of phenomena.**

In this context, the Singaporeans' **Relating Systems** are rated at level 3.0: the citizens learn to share images without the skills to negotiate merged and personalized images of phenomena.

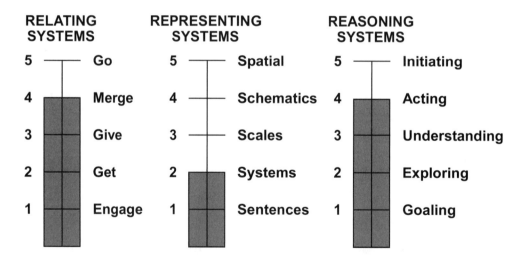

Figure 11. Levels of Generative Thinking Processes

Representing Systems

Perhaps the most demanding requirements for **Generative Thinking** are the **Representing Systems** with which people process. The Singaporeans are, to be sure, advanced conceptually and operationally. However, they lack systematic ways of representing information schematically and spatially (See again Figure 11):

- **Sentences to represent conceptual information;**
- **Systems to represent operational information;**
- **Scaling to represent dimensional information;**
- **Schematics to represent multidimensional information;**
- **Spatial perspectives to represent phenomenal information.**

Accordingly, the Singaporeans' **Representing Systems** are rated at level 2.0: they enable their citizens to design systems and define operations for phenomena; they do not empower their citizens to generate images of scales and schematics, tailored for their own unique purposes.

Reasoning Systems

The culminating phases in **Generative Thinking** are the **Reasoning Systems** that employ the **Representing Systems** to process. The Singaporeans are, once again, advanced in their ability to explore, understand and act upon phenomena. However, they lack the systematic processes for **Reasoning** with **Schematic Information** at all levels (See again Figure 11):

- **Exploring by expanding and analyzing phenomena;**
- **Understanding by narrowing and synthesizing new phenomena;**
- **Acting by doing or operationalizing new objectives;**
- **Initiating by individualizing entrepreneurial initiatives.**

Accordingly, the Singaporeans' **Reasoning Systems** are rated at level 4.0: they enable their citizens to explore by analyzing the operations of phenomena and to understand by synthesizing the systems of new phenomena; they empower their citizens to act to operationalize new objectives, but they do not empower their citizens to initiate entrepreneurially.

To sum, the Singaporeans receive ratings of levels 3, 2, 4 on **Generative Thinking** systems:

- **The capacity to share information by getting and giving images;**

- **The capacity to represent dimensionalized information by systems;**

- **The capacity to reason with information by exploring, understanding and acting upon information operations.**

Again, the good news is that the Singaporeans have addressed the processing of information. The bad news is that they have no systematic ways of processing; indeed, they have no systematic phases for processing. The bottom line is that their processing systems cannot support the continuous generation of **New Capital.**

The Freedom Profile

We may now reflect upon the Singaporean **Freedom-Building Profile. The Collaboration-Driven Freedom Functions** are accomplished by entrepreneurially-architected state positioning in the marketplace that is enabled by sharing processes. In short, Singapore has adopted a collaborative model for social, economic and political growth. Collaboration is its great strength in the respect that Singapore works with others to architect a niche in the marketplace. Collaboration is also a limiting function since Singapore is incapable of generating its own destiny.

Singapore has thrived upon this state-architected entrepreneurial model. It has collaborated with leading **Multinational Corporations** and first-line universities in the transition from information and electronics technologies to pharmaceutical and biotechnologies. In so doing, it has managed to maintain a modal economic growth rate in the nine percent range over three decades, thus doubling the size of its economy every eight to ten years. As an island of 4 million people, it has generated an economy of over $110 billion for a **Per Capita GDP** of over $27,000.

Moreover, defining **Freedom** as the absence of government constraint upon private sector enterprise, The Heritage Foundation has repeatedly designated Singapore among the *"Free Nations"* of the **Global Marketplace.** Nevertheless, The Heritage Foundation still calls Singapore to task for its government-linked companies or **GLCs** as risk-aversive retarders of private sector initiative. To be sure, the state-architected entrepreneurial model allows the system to run in the draft of the world's R & D and economic leaders.

Perhaps the greatest limitation for an enduring socioeconomic growth system is the absence of a supportive culture for generating individual initiatives within the development of **New Capital** and the achievement of **Freedom Functions.** More succinctly, it is the absence of *"True Individual Freedom"* that constitutes the greatest vulnerability in the state-architected collaborative system.

To be more editorial, it is individual risk-aversion that causes Singapore to avoid relating interdependently with other free and diverse cultures!

It is individual risk-aversion that causes Singaporeans to avoid true entrepreneurism in favor of consensus-built industries with profit-built **Multinational Corporations.**

It is individual risk-aversion that causes Singaporeans to avoid the unique interactions of unique individuals who may upset the state planning system that must be maintained at all cost.

Indeed, it is the planning systems of risk-aversion that plant the seeds of control rather than the seeds of freedom.

Singapore is now a **Global Leader.** It has demonstrated the benefits of intelligence in crafting state-sponsored, collaborative organizational initiatives.

Above all else, Singapore has demonstrated intentionality: It can go anywhere it wants to go—it can become anything it wants to be! It knows the formula: **Freedom yields Prosperity!** It need only increase its **Freedom** to increase its **Prosperity!**

Developmentally, Singapore is the exemplary model for all other nations in similar circumstances: It represents a necessary but not sufficient stage of development in a **Possibilities Economy and Civilization.**

4. Hong Kong and Venezuela— For Better or Worse!

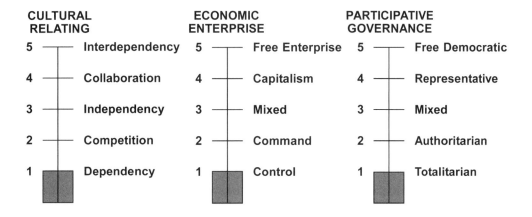

CULTURAL RELATING		ECONOMIC ENTERPRISE		PARTICIPATIVE GOVERNANCE	
5	Interdependency	5	Free Enterprise	5	Free Democratic
4	Collaboration	4	Capitalism	4	Representative
3	Independency	3	Mixed	3	Mixed
2	Competition	2	Command	2	Authoritarian
1	Dependency	1	Control	1	Totalitarian

We may see the differences between **Possibilities Economics** and **Probabilities Economics** in sharp relief by studying two contrasting cultures—Hong Kong and Venezuela—as well as the powerful influences upon them.

Hong Kong ranks among the leaders of the **"Free"** nations evaluated. Long a British protectorate, Hong Kong has elevated its economic freedom under the *"protection"* of the People's Republic of China since 1997. While there have been *"bumps in the road,"* Hong Kong has remained among the world's freest economies as well as its 10th largest trading entity and 11th greatest banking center.

Venezuela, in turn, has been in steep decline since President Hugo Chavez took over and is now ranked among the most *"repressed"* of **"Unfree Nations."** Chavez' concession to Cuba's totalitarian governance and control economics led to a precipitous decline in the economy over the last several years.

The Freedom Functions

The Freedom Functions are the functions to which **Possibilities Economics** is dedicated:

- **Cultural relating with other cultures in the marketplace;**
- **Economic enterprise to generate wealth in the marketplace;**
- **Participative governance to empower enterprise economics in the marketplace.**

Together, these requirements define the requirements of the **21st Century Global Village and Its Marketplace.**

Hong Kong

Hong Kong's levels of **Freedom Functions** may be viewed in Figure 12. As may be noted, Hong Kong's citizenry aspires grandly in an automaton manner as a carry-over from the British:

- **Collaborative Cultural Relating,**
- **Capitalistic Enterprise Economics,**
- **Representative Democratic Governance.**

Accordingly, Hong Kong was rated at 4's on all of **The Freedom Functions.**

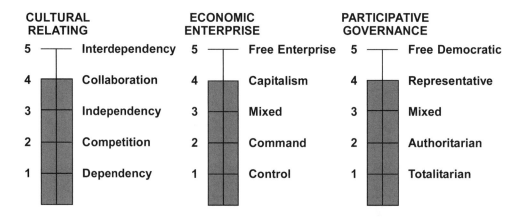

Figure 12. Levels of Freedom Functions (Hong Kong)

While its leadership may aspire to still higher levels, they have not been **"released"** by their **"protector"** to search for higher levels of functioning:

- True interdependency defined by mutual processing for mutual benefit;

- Truly free enterprise defined by entrepreneurial initiative of individuals and small companies rather than intrapreneurial initiative of **Multinational Companies;**

- Truly participative and direct democracy defined by personal communications with the appropriate decision-makers.

Hong Kong's levels of **New Capital Development Components** may be viewed in Figure 13. As may be noted, Hong Kong's leadership implements the following levels of **NCD:**

- **Commercialized-Driven Marketplace Positioning,**
- **Marketing-Driven Organizational Alignment,**
- **Input-Driven Human Processing.**

Accordingly, Hong Kong was rated 3.4.4 on **New Capital Development.**

Figure 13. Levels of NCD (Hong Kong)

Again, while its leadership may aspire to higher levels of **NCD,** it is not yet sophisticated in the operations involved:

- **Generativity** defined by real technological breakthroughs;

- **Leadership** defined by values-based, deductive initiatives;

- **Goaling** defined by values-based decisions in requirement-based markets.

Hong Kong's levels of **Generative Thinking Processes** may be viewed in Figure 14. As may be noted, Hong Kong's rank-and-file thinkers are limited in their **Generative Thinking Skills:**

- **Capable of getting and giving images of information;**

- **Capable of representing images at the systems levels** (although they continue to write reports conceptually at the Sentence Level);

- **Capable of Reasoning with the Images at Operational Levels of Exploring, Understanding and Acting.**

Accordingly, Hong Kong was rated 3.2.4 on **Generative Thinking Systems.**

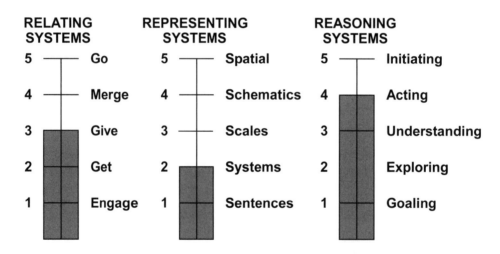

Figure 14. Levels of Thinking (Hong Kong)

Again, while its leadership may aspire to higher levels of thinking, it has not been empowered in their operations. The people know what they are taught and, at best, they emphasize **S–O–R Discriminative Learning Systems.** They do not know what they don't know: **S–P–R Generative Thinking Systems** and more!

Venezuela

Venezuela's levels of **Freedom Functions** are much easier to scale (See Figure 15). As may be noted, the rank-and-file of the people, while many are opposed to a **Totalitarian** takeover, have surrendered to the following:

- **Dependent Adaptive Relating,**
- **Control Economics,**
- **Totalitarian Governance.**

Accordingly, Venezuela was rated at 1s on all of **The Freedom Functions.**

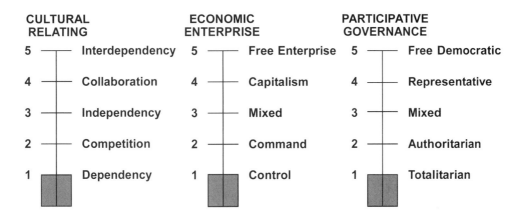

CULTURAL RELATING

5	Interdependency
4	Collaboration
3	Independency
2	Competition
1	Dependency

ECONOMIC ENTERPRISE

5	Free Enterprise
4	Capitalism
3	Mixed
2	Command
1	Control

PARTICIPATIVE GOVERNANCE

5	Free Democratic
4	Representative
3	Mixed
2	Authoritarian
1	Totalitarian

Figure 15. Levels of Freedom Functions (Venezuela)

As a divided country, the people have only **"memory traces"** of their once-proud democratic governance (the first in South America), capitalistic economics (they formed **OPEC** and were the economic leaders of South America), and collaborative cultural relating (they were the freest of the Latin countries).

Venezuela's levels of **New Capital Development Components** may be viewed in Figure 16. As may be noted, Venezuela's citizenry has defaulted on all **NCD:**

- **Driven by Attenuation in the Market** (even in the face of the nation's extraordinary resources!);

- **Reduced to Production Specialties in the Organization** (with limited technologies and declining proficiencies!);

- **Regressed to Planning in Human Processing** (with declining standards of performance!).

Accordingly, Venezuela was rated 1.1.2 on **New Capital Development.**

Figure 16. Levels of NCD (Venezuela)

The truth is this: even with an educated citizenry, Venezuelans were disinclined to employ systematic ways of doing things. They were, as they say jokingly about themselves, blessed with natural resources and **"plagued"** by the human resources who populate the country!

Venezuela's levels of **Generative Thinking Processes** may be viewed in Figure 17. As may be noted, Venezuela's rank-and-file thinkers have never really joined **The Information Age,** let alone **The Ideation Age** required of them now:

- **Capable of getting and giving images of information,**

- **Limited to representing images of information to the conceptual or sentence level,**

- **Incapable of reasoning with images of information beyond the exploring level.**

Accordingly, Venezuela was rated 3.1.2 on **Generative Thinking Processes.**

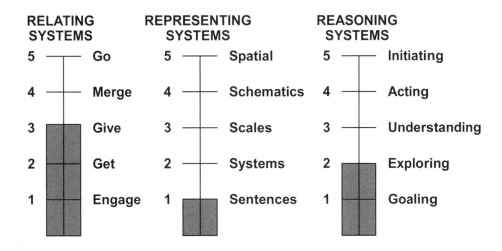

Figure 17. Levels of Thinking (Venezuela)

Again, **we are what we are trained to be**! Historically, while educated classically, Venezuelans were not trained systematically for much! Certainly, not for 21st century thinking! That is precisely why they have been so vulnerable to totalitarian thinking!

What all this means is this:

- Hong Kong has **"thrived"** precariously under the **"protection"** of the People's Republic of China which is, itself, an **"Unfree"** nation.

- Venezuela has dissembled under the direction of Cuba which is, itself, a **"Repressed"** nation (indeed, Cuba has been jockeying historically with North Korea and others for last place among the nations of the world).

In short, **it matters what friends you pick!** Or, in the case of Hong Kong, it matters what friends pick you!

- **Nations that concede to the retarding thinking of Totalitarianism in any form will be retarded! Their peoples will become dependent and controlled by command economics and Totalitarian governance.**

- **Nations that are protected from the retarded thinking of Totalitarianism will be facilitated! Their peoples will become collaborative and released to free enterprise economics and free democratic governance.**

The levels of economic freedom may be viewed in Table 2. As may be noted, there is no overlap between Hong Kong's ratings and the ratings of **"Unfree Nations."** Nevertheless, the People's Republic of China took it upon themselves to **"protect"** Hong Kong's levels of freedom.

Table 2. Levels of Freedom and Prosperity

LEVELS OF FREEDOM
FUNCTIONS

COUNTRY	Cultural Relating	Free Enterprise	Participative Governance	Per Capita* Earnings
Singapore	4.0	4.0	4.0	$27,172
Hong Kong	4.0	4.0	4.0	$24,505
Malaysia	1.0	2.0	1.0	$ 4,708
Venezuela	1.0	1.0	1.0	$ 3,326
China, PRC	1.0	1.0	1.0	$ 925
Cuba	1.0	1.0	1.0	$ N/A **

*Per Capita GDP is estimated in 1995 Constant U.S. Dollars.
**Not Applicable. Per Capita GDP for Cuba estimated from 2003 Purchasing Power Parity is $1,700.

In turn, the mentoring relationship between Cuba and Venezuela proved a retarding one for Venezuela. That's because the concession was from Venezuela to Cuba—from democracy to totalitarianism, from mixed economic enterprise to control economics. Of all the countries in the world, Venezuela has had the greatest decline in all **Freedoms** over the last ten years. That is because Cuba has introduced **"The Totalitarian Protocol:"** first, scare the upper class so it leaves; second, intimidate the middle class so it is reduced to the underclass; third, elevate the underclass through promotion and subsidization.

The consequences are found in the per capita **GDP** of the countries involved. Venezuela's per capita earnings have had a precipitous decline from over $8,000 in 1999 to approximately $3,000 in 2002, with current estimates nearing the $1,000 level. Meanwhile, Hong Kong's citizens are approaching $25,000 per capita.

This analysis is further bolstered by the achievements of another leader among **"Free"** nations. Emerging from **Authoritarian Governance, Control Economics** and **Dependent Relating,** Singapore has become a leader in **Collaborative Cultural Relating, Capitalistic Economics** and **Representative Governance.** Today, Singapore has **Freedom Profiles** and earnings directly comparable with Hong Kong. Where Hong Kong did so as an historic *"protectorate,"* Singapore did so with existential intentionality!

Moreover, we may view the economic progress of Malaysia, another **"Unfree"** nation that originally rejected unification with Singapore because of their discrimination against Cultural Chinese leadership. We discover huge differences in per capita **GDP:** over $27,000 for Singaporeans and under $5,000 for Malaysians. Again, Singapore refused to be derailed by the rejection of a nation with six times the population and many hundreds of times the size and natural resources.

From a scientific perspective, then, we have several studies operating:

- Singapore is dramatically improved in **Freedom** with a **GDP** that is doubling nearly every ten years;

- Hong Kong is still attempting to elevate its economic **Freedoms** and earnings in a precariously **"protective"** relationship with an **"Unfree Nation;"**

- Venezuela is deteriorating in **Freedom** and earnings in a retarding relationship with a **"Repressed"** dictatorship.

In transition, **Freedom-Building** is about change. Once we let this genie out of the bottle, we can never get it back, except under extreme conditions of harsh **Totalitarianism** in governance, crude control in economics, and oppressed dependency in cultural relating. The ultimate battle of the human condition is **Freedom versus Totalitarianism.**

The very term, **"conditions,"** determined the conditioning of our past. Even now the conditioning of the present takes countries like Cuba and Venezuela into the oblivion of the **Totalitarian** human condition.

In a similar manner, the conditions of **Freedom** generate the opportunities of the future. Leaders like Lee and Goh have empowered the people of Singapore to move with intentionality from a **Totalitarian** past to an **Egalitarian** future.

Even Hong Kong, with its rich history of freedom, has been treated **"protectively"** by the mandates of the **"Unfree"** People's Republic of China, seemingly as China's experiment for becoming **"Free"** on its own terms and in its own way.

Change begins with empowering individuals with **Generative Thinking Systems:**

- **Relating** to receive all ideas;
- **Representing** to image all ideas;
- **Reasoning** to generate new and better ideas.

By empowering individuals with **Generative Thinking Skills,** we have prepared them for the **21st Century Global Village.**

Changes are multiplied exponentially in organizations, communities and cultures that generate all forms of **New Capital Development** or **NCD:**

- **Marketplace Positioning** or **MCD,**
- **Organizational Alignment** or **OCD,**
- **Human Processing** or **HCD,**
- **Information Modeling** or **ICD,**
- **Mechanical Tooling** or **mCD.**

By empowering these socioeconomic institutions and the people in them with **NCD,** we have prepared them for the 21st century global marketplace.

Changes culminate in the marketplace. Indeed, they culminate over and over every minute with the trillions of decisions made each day in the marketplace. By empowering the participants in the marketplace—individuals, organizations, communities, cultures—in **The Freedom Functions,** they move toward becoming generators of those very sources of change:

- **Interdependent Cultural Relating,**
- **Free Enterprise Economics,**
- **Free Democratic Governance.**

With **The Freedom Functions,** we will all be peaceful, prosperous and progressive.

Economic growth and wealth are made possible by reorienting ourselves to new and more powerful definitions of the skills and systems of **New Capital Development.**

It is time to abandon the exclusiveness of **The Old Probabilities Economy** because it has already abandoned us:

- Built as it is upon false assumptions of the scarcity of finite resources;
- Focused as it is around superstitious indices of central tendency and variability;
- Supported as it is by artificial interventions of simulated potency!

Economics is simply not about **Financial Capital,** important catalytic agent that it is. Our economies simply cannot be sustained, let alone grow, by minor movements in prime interest rates, tax rebates and defense spending. When we are manipulating minor interventions within the 15% of variability in **Economic Growth** accounted for by **Financial Capital,** then our economic benefits are, at best, miniscule and, at worst, infinitesimal.

Certainly, there may be short-term economic movement based upon phenomenal or psychological benefits. However, when the longer-term expectancies are not met, the artificial interventions may, in fact, operate as **"depressor variables",** actually depressing economic performance.

Without new ingredients, there is no economic movement! Without substance, there are no new ingredients! Substance will be found in **New Capital Development!**

In this context, **Freedom** generates an **Economy of Increasing Abundance:**

- **An Abundance of Intelligence,**
- **An Abundance of Prosperity,**
- **An Abundance of Change.**

Freedom generates **The Possibilities Economy.**

It will empower us to fulfill our destinies: To become growing humans in sane and evolving civilized societies!

In transition, **The Freedom Wars** are about how we treat the exemplary performers whom others would emulate. The **"Free"** nations build them. The **Totalitarians** attack them.

III. The Freedom Paradigms

5. U.S.A. — The Generative Innovator

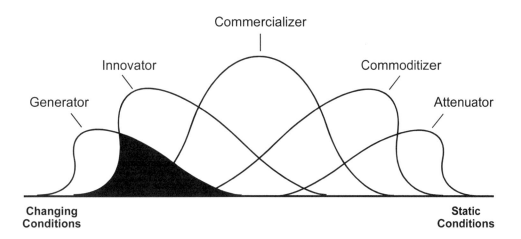

The market curve is not a normal curve. Indeed, nothing in God's universes is linear, normal and symmetrical. To be sure, the so-called market curve is comprised of multiple market curves: it is multi-modal. Each curve, in turn, is multidimensional, interdependent and curvilinear as well as asymmetrical and changeable. We may view a representation of these market curves as follows:

- **Generating or stimulating markets through breakthroughs;**
- **Innovating or initiating markets through transfers;**
- **Commercializing or culminating markets through consumer-responsiveness;**
- **Commoditizing or draining markets through producing more for less;**
- **Attenuating or breaking markets through product *"dumping."***

For our purposes, we label these market phases **"GICCA."** They have profound implications for their nations, cultures, people and products. They dominate **The Global Marketplace.**

The market curves are stimulated by the technological breakthroughs of the **Generator. The Generator Curve** is tilted toward changing conditions and skewed away from static conditions. This means that the culture and its people and the products are oriented to changing conditions, either by responding to existing needs or creating needs for future conditions. In this respect, the **Generator Cultures** are beyond any existing market curves and before any new markets. Indeed, they exist in a *"limbo"* of **"Pre-Market Conditions,"** often residing only in the minds of their inventors.

The real market curves do not come into being until the **Innovators** step into the picture. **The Innovator Curve** is tilted toward the substance of the **Generator** and the changing conditions of the marketplace. This means that the **Innovator Culture** has one eye on the ideas of the **Generator** and the other eye on the potential of the marketplace. In this respect, the **Innovators** initiate the market curves.

More than anyone else, they are responsible for the creation of the commercial markets.

The **Commercializers** are, of course, those responsible for *"peaking"* the market curves. **The Commercializer Curve** is directed straight to customer needs in order to achieve the indices of robust sales. This means that the **Commercializer Cultures** have both eyes on maximizing the indices of market commerciality: productivity, gross, profit, growth, market share. In this respect, the **Commercializers** *are* the **Commercial Market:** they produce more so that they can profit more!

The appearance of the **Commoditizers** are early warnings of the decline of the commercial market. Indeed, often the **Commoditizers** cause the decline of the **Commercial Market:** they produce more for less! **The Commoditizer Curve** is tilted toward the static conditions of the marketplace and away from changing conditions. As such, the **Commoditizer Cultures** seek the security of expanding sales even in the face of declining profits.

Ultimately, the **Attenuators** take over this decline. This curve is skewed away from change. The **Attenuator Curve** is a curve of attenuating benefits: producing more and more for less and less. The apparent stability sought by the **Attenuator Cultures** is undermined by the ultimate reductionistic **Principle of Attenuation:** *producing everything for nothing!*

The issues of globalization, jobs and education for the 21st century **Global Economy** converge upon the phases of **The GICCA Curve.** Succinctly, all of these issues would be resolved in continuous and interdependent processing for a bountiful and expanding future with the continuation of **"The GIC Relationships:"**

- **Generative** or **"breakthrough"** research by the likes of IBM's Watson Center and the old AT&T's Bell Labs;

- **Innovative** contextual **"transfers"** of these breakthroughs by laboratory-based industries such as Microsoft and Intel;

- **Commercial** applications of these innovations by consumer-responsive businesses such as General Electric and Westinghouse.

These **"GIC Relationships"** sustained and grew the American economy throughout the second half of the 20th century. Unfortunately, they no longer relate, let alone process collaboratively. Due in large part to the American business reaction to the Japanese *"blind-siding"* of the 1980's, American businesses retreated from *generating* to *innovating* in order to defeat *imitating*. There are no longer any R & D centers of any consequence: there is little scientific search, let alone research, to explicate the unknown; only developmental trials to prepare **"pilots"** *for* commercialization.

Moreover, by abdicating systematic **"GIC"** leadership, the U.S.A. has slowed world **Generativity** down to a random trickle. Not only has the U.S. suffered from short-term stasis, but the nations of the world will now suffer from long-term paralysis as the wheels of **Generativity** grind to a halt. Concurrently, both leader and followers are surrendering to **Multinational Corporations** that sponsor little **Generativity** and have no alignment with **American Civilization** other than capitalistic profitability.

In this context, the U.S. is the hope — not only for its citizenry — but for the peoples of the world. Indeed, the U.S. is **The Multicultural "Experiment for the World:"** if things work there, they can work anywhere. An essay by Rob Owen may suffice as an introduction to the American system.

The Great Experiments

In the history of humankind, there have been three great movements in freedom for civilization and its people. Each constitutes a vital experiment in the realization of human potential.

The First Experiment — Ancient Greece

The first freedom movement was embodied in the government of Pericles in ancient Greece. Schooled in the writings of Greek philosophers such as Plato and Aristotle, Pericles demonstrated that true democracy was possible. Although his demonstration was fatally flawed by the system of slavery upon which Greek democracy was based, it was an initial step toward a new view of government and citizenry. As such, it was **The First Experiment in Freedom.** And it was validated!

The Great Experiment — The United States

The second great movement was the American system, founded more than 200 years ago. Basing their ideas upon the work of European philosophers such as John Locke, Thomas Hobbes, and David Hume, the founders of this system demonstrated that not only democratic governance was possible, but free enterprise economics as well.

Of course, the American system was also flawed by withholding full freedoms and rights from First Americans, women, Blacks, and other marginalized peoples. However, this flaw was not a fatal one. Our founders were politically conscious enough to give us an amending instrument to enact changes in the movement toward full freedom: the U.S. Constitution. The equality of all "men" having been declared, it remained for the disenfranchised to seek and achieve their own civil and human rights through amendments to the Constitution.

Indeed, today the U.S. stands alone as the beacon of freedom in the world:

- Its 50 states, some of them larger than countries, live together peacefully and productively in the freest social system the world.

- Its 50 states, many of which would be among the most prosperous of countries, conduct the freest and most powerful wealth-generating economic system in the history of the world. The citizens of its 50 states are constitutionally the policymakers of the freest representative democratic governance of the most powerful nation in the history of the world.

The U.S. has truly demonstrated itself to be **The Great Experiment.** And it has been validated!

The Next Great Experiment — Free Global Society

Evolving in our times, the third freedom movement is represented by **The Freedom Doctrine,** which offers a futuristic vision of the global village and its marketplace. Informed by the spiraling achievements of the American experiment, **The Freedom Doctrine** points civilization toward an elevated and integrated global society based upon the fundamental proposition of **Global Freedom:** *"All nations are created equal in their potential for freedom."* The functions of such freedom include:

- **Free and interdependent cultural relating,**
- **Entrepreneurially driven, free enterprise economics,**
- **Free and direct democratic governance.**

The methods for achieving these **Freedom Functions** tell the story of **The Freedom Doctrine.**

We are thus called to engage in **The Next Great Experiment**— to build our people, our communities, all cultures, and all nations into an elevated, integrated, and interdependent global society. This is **The Freedom Doctrine,** and it will be validated again and again (Owen, Foreword in *The Freedom Doctrine,* pp. ix–x).

This brief introduction brings us to **The Freedom Functions** where the U.S. is unparalleled in its historic performance:

- **Cultural Relating** where 50 large states of diverse cultures have lived collaboratively in peace and harmony for nearly 150 years.

- **Free Enterprise** where the state economies rank among the largest in the world and converge to produce an American economy of 11 trillion that is as large as the combined total of the next four nations (there are no *real* competitors!).

- **Participative Governance** where American citizens are, themselves, defined by the U.S. Constitution to be the policymakers of the greatest democracy the world has ever known.

These nonpareil performances serve to introduce an operational analysis of **The Freedom Functions.**

The Freedom Functions

The first decisions were not made by our forefathers as systematically as we may now make them. They simply implemented the philosophies of **The Great Western Minds** who conceived of **The Great Experiment.** Over two centuries, the U.S. defined the emerging requirements of **The Global Marketplace:**

- **Free Cultural Relating,**
- **Free Enterprise Economics,**
- **Free Participative Governance.**

These are the requirements for entry into the 21st century marketplace. They also define the **American Mission.**

Cultural Relating

Simply stated, a nation must relate culturally — within, between and among cultures — in order to join **The Global Marketplace.** American leaders have always set their goals high on **Cultural Relating** (See Figure 18). Even when they retreat to independency or, in the case of The War on Terrorism, competitiveness, they never surrender the ideas of collaborative relating. While their definitions of interdependency may be shallow, they are nevertheless striving toward it.

In short, the U.S. is rated at level 4.0 on **Cultural Relating,** reflecting its commitment to collaboration without real motivation for interdependency (perhaps as a function of the conflict of individualism with consensus), except within rare homogeneous cultural groupings.

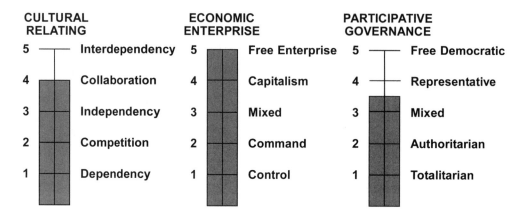

Figure 18. Levels of The Freedom Functions

Economic Enterprise

The U.S.A. is dedicated to **Free Enterprise** at the highest levels. Succinctly, the U.S. Constitution, protecting private property and, in an amended form, civil and economic liberties, provides a strong foundation for the nation's free and dynamic economy. In addition, the U.S. has taken the leadership in promoting free trade, not only with neighbors in the Western Hemisphere but with nations around the world. While not yet having realized its mission of **Universal Free Enterprise,** the U.S. is the world leader, par excellence.

In short, the U.S. is rated at level 5.0 on **Free Enterprise,** reflecting its aspirations for reciprocal trade at the highest levels (See again Figure 18). Whatever the obstacles and however they are resolved through **Collaborative Processing,** there would be no vision of **The Global Marketplace** without America's highly initiative leadership; there would be no standards for **Prosperity** and, thus, for the evolution of the **American** and **World Civilization!**

Participative Governance

The U.S. has also been dedicated to **Participative Governance** at high levels. While its citizens are guaranteed pre-potent policymaking functions by the U.S. Constitution, its representative democracy often migrates into a *"role reversal"* where citizens serve politicians and bureaucrats. Nowhere has American promotion of democracy been more problematic than in attempts to impose it upon foreign cultures such as Iraq, where, for example, Mormon missionaries were sponsored to teach U.S. Constitutional law to Muslim Mullahs. Participating begins with relating to other's frames of reference before empowering them to achieve their own unique purposes. That is the true nature of democracy. There is no freedom without empowerment! There is no empowerment without relating!

In short, the U.S. is rated at level 3.5 on **Participative Governance** (See again Figure 18), reflecting the inconsistent nature of its attempts at making representative governance work; stumbling that leads precipitously to representative self-aggrandizement; stumbling that yields disastrously to authoritarianism by default.

To sum, the U.S. receives variable ratings on relating, enterprise and governance:

- **Collaborative Relating,**
- **Free Enterprise Economics,**
- **Mixed Representative and Authoritarian Governance.**

The good news is that, however *"ugly"* externally, the U.S. continues to relate collaboratively internally and with friends and neighbors. Moreover, the U.S. is convergent externally and internally with its path-finding **Free Enterprise Mission.** The bad news is that, while projecting the democratic image in an authoritarian manner externally, meaningful participative governance is dissembling internally.

New Capital Components

The means to accomplishing **The Freedom Functions** are **The New Capital Development** or **NCD Components:**

- **MCD**—Marketplace Capital Development or Marketplace Positioning;

- **OCD**—Organizational Capital Development or Organizational Alignment with MCD Positioning;

- **HCD**—Human Capital Development or Empowered Human Processing to implement OCD Alignment;

- **ICD**—Information Capital Development or Information Modeling to implement HCD Processing;

- **mCD**—Mechanical Capital Development or Mechanical Tooling to implement ICD Modeling.

Together, these **Components** define the **New Capital Development** required to achieve and elevate **The Freedom Functions.**

We may view the levels of **NCD Components** in Figure 19. As may be noted, the U.S. rates at or near the highest levels of all of these **NCD Systems:**

- **MCD Positioning** driven by **Generative Marketplace Positioning (Level 5);**

- **OCD Alignment** driven by **Marketing Systems (Level 4);**

- **HCD Processing** driven by **Inputting Systems (Level 4);**

- **ICD Modeling** driven by **Vectorial Systems (Level 4);**

- **mCD Tooling** driven by **Operational Systems (Level 5).**

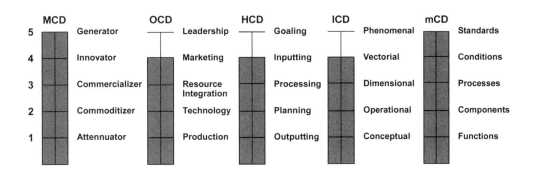

Figure 19. Levels of NCD Components

Together, these **NCD Components** provide the U.S. with the **New Capital** it requires to achieve and elevate **The Freedom Functions.** Unfortunately, the **OCD, HCD** and **ICD Systems** are limiting factors on fully robust **NCD.**

Generative Thinking Processes

The processes that empower or enable **The NCD Components** to accomplish **The Freedom Functions** are **The Generative Thinking Processes** or **Possibilities Thinking Systems:**

- **Relating Systems** that enable people to receive and negotiate images of information;

- **Representing Systems** that enable people to represent images of information;

- **Reasoning Systems** that enable people to generate improved images of information and entrepreneurial initiatives.

Together, these processes define the **Generative Thinking Processes** necessary to enable **The NCD Components** to achieve **The Freedom Functions.**

We may view the levels of **Generative Processes** in Figure 20. As may be noted, the people of the U.S. rate variably on the **Generative Thinking Systems:**

- **Merging-driven** or consensus levels of images of information (Level 4);

- **Systems-driven** levels of representing images of information (Level 2);

- **Action-driven** levels of reasoning with images of information (Level 4).

Together, **The Generative Thinking Processes** are calculated to enable **The NCD Components** to achieve **The Freedom Functions.** Unfortunately, the limitations of **Systems Representing** inhibit **Reasoning** from achieving the highest levels of **Entrepreneurial Initiative.**

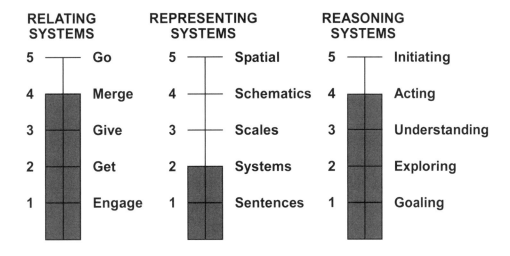

Figure 20. Levels of Generative Thinking Processes

The American Enterprise Model

The American Enterprise Model may be viewed in Figure 21. This model is the generative source of **The American Enterprise Systems** that elevate the U.S. to path-finder in the marketplace.

As may be noted, **The Freedom Functions** are dominated by **Free Enterprise:**

- **Free Enterprise Economics** are the **Functions** of the **American Freedom Mission.**

- **Mixed Representative** and **Authoritarian Governance** are the **Empowering/ Limiting Freedom Components.**

- **Collaborative Cultural Relating** is the **Enabling Process** for the **Empowering Components.**

In other words, **Cultural Relating** and **Participative Governance** are the enabling and empowering systems supporting the achievement of **Free Enterprise** at the highest levels. Unfortunately, the supportive governance systems are currently inadequate to sustain **The Free Enterprise Mission.**

In turn, **The NCD Components** are driven by **Generative Positioning:**

- Generative **MCD Positioning,**
↓
- Marketing-driven **OCD Alignment,**
↓
- Input-driven **HCD Processing,**
↓
- Vectorial-driven **ICD Modeling,**
↓
- Standards-driven **mCD Tooling.**

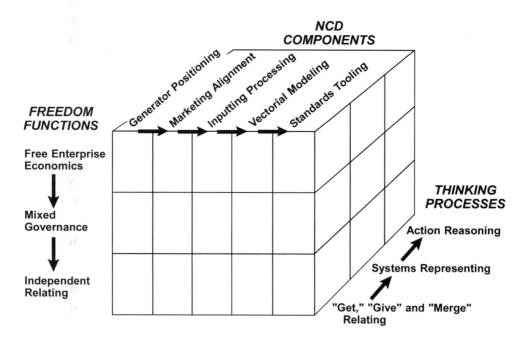

Figure 21. The American Enterprise Model

Together, these **NCD Systems** are dedicated to implementing **The Generative MCD Positioning** and accomplishing **The Freedom Functions.** Unfortunately, the **OCD, HCD,** and **ICD systems** are functioning below the high levels required by **The Generative Positioning.**

Finally, **The Generative Thinking Processes** are dominated by **Action Objectives:**

- **Relating** to negotiate merged images of information;
- **Representing** systems' images of information;
- **Reasoning** to generate improved images for acting.

Together, **"The New 3Rs of Thinking"** generate the **Action Images** that enable **The NCD Components** to achieve **The Freedom Functions.** Unfortunately, the **Systems Representations** place a lid upon the **Reasoning** requirements for **Entrepreneurial Initiative.**

We may summarize an operational definition of the **American Enterprise Model:**

> **Free Enterprise-driven Functions** are accomplished by **Generator-driven NCD Components** enabled by **Action-driven Generative Thinking Processes.**

So long as Americans understand the implications of both the assets and deficits of this **Generative Enterprise Model,** they can empower **The American Systems** to continue to lead the world to **The 21st Century Global Marketplace.**

The implications for **The Freedom Functions** are obvious and profound:

- Empower **Free Enterprise** with the levels of **Cultural Relating** and **Participative Governance Support Systems** required for **The 21st century Global Marketplace!**

- Rehabilitate the **Governance Systems** with **Direct Democratic Relating (Electronically)** and replace the *"Turkey's who gobble locally but can't fend globally!"*

- Elevate **Cultural Relating** to a **Human Processing "Art-Form"** in order to achieve the benefits of **Interdependent Processing with Diverse Cultures!**

Accomplishing these improvements will empower **The Generativity-driven NCD** to accomplish **The Free Enterprise Mission.**

The Generative Innovator

The **American Enterprise** positioning on **The GICCA Curve** can be seen most clearly in Figure 22. As may be noted, the historic **"GIC Relationship"** is at risk: the **Generators** who drove the American economy upward and outward throughout the 20th century are no longer supported: business enterprises no longer have an interest in problematic, long-term commercial payoffs on investments. With **Generative-Innovator Positioning, The Innovation-Commercialization Cycle** is accelerated and the longer-term opportunities for American job opportunities and career fulfillment are diminished. Basically, as the work shifts from piloting to standardizing, the positions are automated and **"farmed out"** to other, more economical business environments. This creates an imbalance of both jobs and justice in the marketplace: those who generate and empower, are punished by losing their jobs!

This imbalance is not the fault of Third World Nations who were never empowered to become reciprocal partners: they have received no training for empathy or reciprocity! This imbalance is the fault of conditioned, linear thinking policymakers who believe that they can go simultaneously in two directions: toward **Globalization** in the interests of **Multinational Corporations** and toward job opportunities in the interests of **"Local-Nationals."** These directions are mutually exclusive without new ingredients or interventions.

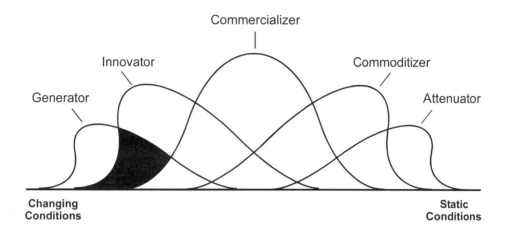

Figure 22. Generative-Innovator Positioning

The critical new interventions are always the same: **Empowerment Through Education and Training, the Pre-Potent Sources of Economic Growth.** Unfortunately, the educational and training systems are architected by the same conditioned, linear thinkers that conduct foreign policy and education. These executives already have the learners and trainees excelling in the same conditioned, linear thinking that enabled the executives to lead America astray. Indeed, the **"Standards-of-Learning"** programs are preparing the learners for the **S–R Conditioned Responding** requirements of **The Industrial Age:** the very same **Conditioning Systems** that enable Third-World workers to take over their assembly-line jobs.

To be sure, the necessary functional and structural changes that enable **Globalization** are clear: **Eliminate the "educators" and elevate the education!** The educational and training experiences must be elevated, minimally, to the **S–O–R Discriminative Learning** and, maximally, to the **S–P–R Generative Processing.** (Later on, we will learn more about higher levels of **Generative Processing.**)

To sum, the U.S. cannot expand its **Globalization Initiatives** while undermining its **Generativity** emphasis in both **R & D** and **E & T**— education and training. To eliminate higher order processing through lack of support and intention is to undermine the fundamental values of the very **Generative Enterprise Model** that made it possible.

A final moral note: It would be an unmitigated disaster for the U.S. to fail in its **Generative Enterprise Leadership.** Should other more homogeneous nations, by default, assume leadership as they attempted in the 20th century, the **March of Civilization** would not only be interrupted but defeated by classist, racist , sexist, and superstitious **"Pirouettes to Discrimination!"** In this context, all **"isms"** are related in a cluster of discriminatory and destructive behaviors.

We will rest our case and, hopefully, stimulate more generative processing on **The American Enterprise Model** by presenting the statement below. Do not blame the messenger! In spite of his grandiosity in imitating potency and his contempt for the sources of his growth, he is only stating what is already known throughout the world.

> Zhu Min, general manager of the state-owned Bank of China, suggested that the U.S. does need "to reposition itself. Manufacturing is gone; services are going. Research and development is still there. [The U.S.] needs to move up the [development] chain."
>
> – *Wall Street Journal,* January 26, 2004

5. U.S.A.—The Generative Innovator

6. Japan—The Innovative Commercializer

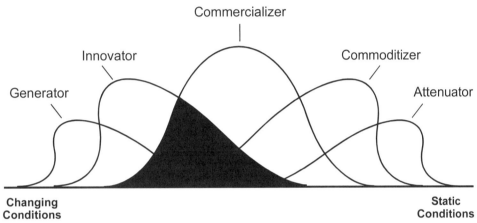

Japan is not really an **Innovator.** It does not meet the standards of the definition:

> *Innovation involves the transfer of all functions, components, processes, conditions and standards of Generative Breakthroughs.*

Indeed, Japan has neither the models and technologies nor the willingness to take the risks of a **True Innovator.** It runs in *"the draft"* of **The Generator.** But it does not pay the price of **Innovation!** In Oscar Wilde's terms, *"It knows the price of everything and the value of nothing."*

Japan seeks only to make the most *"cost-effective"* commercial transfers, those of conditions or contexts. To be sure, its historic success has been to influence the world to conceive of transfer as **"Contextual"** in nature. That is why the Japanese surround every patent with an absurd number of applications for **"Contextual Transfers."** It is as if they may never get another idea!

Yes, Japan is not really an **Innovator.** It is a **"Wannabe"** that wins the **"Innovator"** title because there are no other applicants for the position.

The Contextual Transfer

The entire modern history of Japan may be encapsulated in the term, **"Contextual Transfer."** Their initial opposition to **"Inferior Civilizations with Superior Technologies"** gives way to the adaptation of the technologies and, reluctantly, the adoption of some aspects of the civilization. In the interim, the nation struggles desperately to reconcile defending a culture designed for another era, while acquiring the commercial technologies of this era.

The senior author has had direct experiences introducing Japan in 1989 to the emergence of **Human Technology** and **Human Capital** as pre-potent ingredients in the equation of economic growth. Without real definition from the author, and without acquisition and application of the skills by the audience, **The Ministry of International Trade and Industry** or **MITI** announced the ultimate **"Contextual Transfer" Industrial Policy:**

> *That Japan would dominate the 21st century economy because of superior **Human Capital** defined by their homogeneous population.*

Incredible as it seems, 15 months after being introduced for the first time to the concept—not the operations—of **"Human Capital,"** MITI had made a **"Contextual Transfer"** that redefined all **Human Capital Operations:**

- The Functions of **"Improved Ideation"** were replaced by **"The Domination of Japan."**

- The Components of **"Diverse and Heterogeneous Human Capital"** were displaced by **"The Homogeneous Japanese Populations."**

- The Processes of **"Generative Thinking"** were redefined as **"Consensus-Building."**

- The Conditions of **"The Global Marketplace"** were eclipsed by **"Market Share."**

The only operation **MITI** forgot was **"Standards."** And you cannot define anything without standards!

Standards enable us to measure our accomplishments. They tell us whether we got to where we said we did. They tell us whether this is just more superstitious mythology or truly superior methodology.

The Japanese Miracle

Japan is a miracle: a medieval culture competing in **The 21ˢᵗ Century Global Marketplace.** This is a real tribute to **The Imitators** and **The Innovators** and **"The Contextual Transfers"** that they make as well as the energy, will and discipline of the Japanese people.

Japan's recovery from the profound destruction of World War II is, itself, an incredible story. The confrontation with American weaponry and standards-of-living brought them **"Culture Shock:"** they were now rewarded for the individualism and expressiveness that they had previously been punished for; they were now punished for the mystical beliefs of the secretive societies that they had previously been rewarded for.

In the 1950s, **"The Economic Miracle"** began to take shape as sustained economic growth became the national mission. Hayato Ikeda summed it all up when **"being demoted"** from **Minister of MITI** to **Prime Minister of Japan:**

> *"Isn't it all a matter of economic policy? I'll go for income doubling."*

Accordingly, **"Japan, Inc."** implemented *"a very effective catch-up model"* with **MITI**-driven economic expansion.

By the 1980s, Japan had begun its shift from an energy-intensive manufacturing economy to a **"Knowledge-Intensive Economy,"** as it aligned with the **American IT Movement.** Viewing itself as a **"Superpower,"** Japan dedicated itself to trading in the world's economy, benefiting enormously from increasing trade with America, its mentor.

Then the *"bubble burst!"* If you run in another's draft, you may catch a cold. The bubble was built upon spiraling stock market and fantasized real estate values in the face of an increasingly sluggish economy.

The resulting slump has extended into the 21ˢᵗ century. Where **"Japan, Inc."** once saw itself as **"Market Leader of the 21ˢᵗ Century,"** it now came to be viewed by **Capital Markets** as **"Market Pariah."**

"Japan, Inc." has no alternatives to change. *"How to change"* is the great internal debate. The success of the relationships between the nation and the marketplace will probably continue to roil. However, the historic wars of **Culture Versus Commercialization** will ultimately be decided by the Japanese people, not so much by their disposition to **Capitalistic Economics** as by their readiness for **The Other Freedom Functions** of **Collaborative Cultural Relating** and **Truly Free Democratic Governance.**

The Freedom Functions

Indeed, the Japanese people must now answer the following questions:

- **Collaborative Cultural Relating? How much?**
- **Free Enterprise Economics? How far?**
- **Free Democratic Governance? How little?**

The answers will dictate Japan's level of membership in **The Global Marketplace.**

Cultural Relating

"Japan, Inc." relates in an **Independent** and **Authoritarian** manner to all peoples—within, between and among cultures. Externally, this is due to its **"Assumed Superiority."** Internally, this is due to its predilection to favor **Authoritarian Governance** over **Individualistic Enterprise.**

In short, Japan is rated generously at Level 3.0 on **Cultural Relating,** reflecting its **Self-Perception of Independence.** This allows it to **"Collaborate-Up"** (to **Favorable Trading Partners** such as the U.S.) and **"Compete-Down"** to the rest of the world, especially its **"Asian Inferiors** (See Figure 23)."

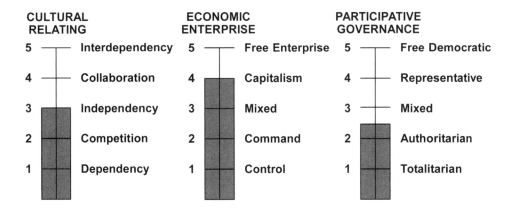

Figure 23. Levels of The Freedom Functions

Economic Enterprise

"**Japan, Inc.**" rates highest on **Economic Enterprise.** It is dedicated to **The Capitalistic Economics** that shaped its **"Miraculous Past."** However, it is conflicted on the model that will empower it to have a **"Miraculous Future."** Indeed, it cannot tolerate the idea of operating without a **Fixed Objective,** a **Static Model** and a **Perseverating Plan.** To be sure, it cannot tolerate the evolving paradigm for embracing **The 21st Century Global Marketplace: "Continuous Interdependent Processing"** within, between and among cultures.

In this context, Japan is rated at level 4.0 on **Economic Enterprise,** reflecting its aspirations to **Commercialize Capitalistically** at the highest levels (See again Figure 23).

Participative Governance

While Japan is a **Constitutional Democracy,** its real business is conducted by **"The Iron Triangle"** of bureaucrats, businessmen, and *"bumbling politicians."* Consequently, aside from **"make believe"** elections, the people have relatively little say about the conduct of governance.

In this context, Japan is rated at level 2.5 for **Participative Governance,** reflecting a continuing tendency to authoritarianism in a classist, sexist and racist society (See again Figure 23).

To sum, Japan receives highly variable ratings on relating, enterprising and governing:

- **Independent Relating,**
- **Capitalistic Economics,**
- **Mixed Governance.**

The bad news is that Japan is not ready to truly *"embrace"* **The Global Marketplace** and its members. The good news is that the Japanese people have always managed to make **"Miraculous Recoveries"** from the incredibly stupid delusions of a **"Malefic Culture."**

New Capital Components

The means of accomplishing **The Freedom Functions** are **The New Capital** or **NCD Components:**

- **MCD** or **Marketplace Positioning;**
- **OCD** or **Organizational Alignment;**
- **HCD** or **Human Processing;**
- **ICD** or **Information Modeling;**
- **mCD** or **Mechanical Tooling.**

Like John T. Kelly says:

> *"These NCD Components apply for everyone. They are requirements. There should be no conflict as to whether to acquire or apply them."*

Relatedly, we may view Japan's level of functioning on **The NCD Components** in Figure 24. As may be noted, Japan rates at highly variable levels:

- **Innovative Commercializer Positioning** (Level 3.5 **MCD**);
- **Marketing-Driven Alignment** (Level 4.0 **OCD**);
- **Input-Driven Human Processing** (Level 4.0 **HCD**);
- **Operations-Driven Information Modeling** (Level 2.0 **ICD**);
- **Standards-Driven Mechanical Tooling** (Level 5.0 **mCD**).

Together, these **NCD Components** provide the foundation for accomplishing **The Elusive and Illusory Innovator Mission.** Unfortunately, the **ICD Systems** are inadequate to the tasks of fulfilling **NCD.**

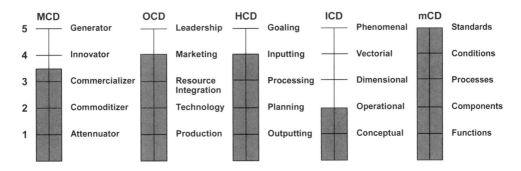

Figure 24. Levels of NCD Components

Generative Thinking Processes

Finally, the processes that empower **The NCD Components** to accomplish **The Freedom Functions** are **The Generative Thinking Processes** or **Possibilities Thinking Systems:**

- **Relating Systems,**
- **Representing Systems,**
- **Reasoning Systems.**

Together, these processes define **The Generative Thinking Systems** necessary to enable **The NCD Components** to achieve **The Freedom Functions.**

We may view the levels of **Generative Processes** in Figure 25. As may be noted, the Japanese people vary widely on **The Generative Thinking Systems:**

- They *"peak"* at **Merging** or **Consensus-Building** (Level 4.0).
- They *"trough"* at **Systems Representing** (Level 2.0).
- They are driven by **Action-Reasoning** (Level 4.0).

The handicap in empowering **NCD Components** is clearly the limited level of **Systems Representing.**

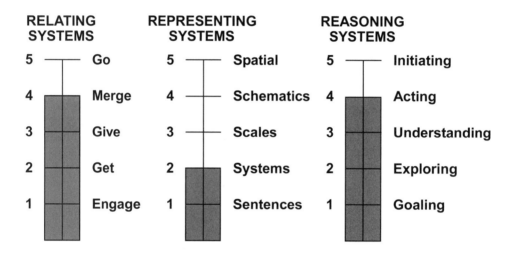

Figure 25. Levels of Generative Thinking Processes

The Japanese Enterprise Model

The **Japanese Enterprise Model** may be viewed in Figure 26. This model is the dominating force in Japanese relations in **The Global Marketplace.**

As may be noted, **The Freedom Functions** are dominated by **Capitalistic Enterprise:**

- **Capitalistic Economics** are **The Functions of the Japanese Mission.**

- **Mixed Representative** and **Authoritarian Governance** are the **Empowering Components.**

- **Independent Cultural Relating** constitutes the **Enabling Processes** for the **Empowering Components.**

As may also be noted, there is only one direction of flow: components and processes are driven by **Capitalist Economic Functions.**

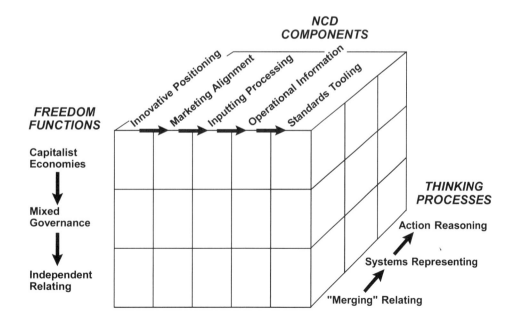

Figure 26. The Japanese Enterprise Model

The problems in the secret agenda of **"Catching the Leader"** are multiple:

- The **Freedom Functions,** under the dictatorship of **Capitalism,** do not interrelate; e.g., there is no interaction or *"two-way street."*

- The functions are inadequate:

  - **Independency** is not a **Relating Function. It is an Oxymoron! "Superior People" simply do not relate!**

  - **Mixed Governance is a Myth. In "Japan, Inc.,"** what this means follows: *"We are democratic until we need to be authoritarian."*

  - **Capitalism is narrowly defined. "Japan, Inc."** does not understand the constructs of **The New Capitalism.** Consequently, it continues to fail in seeking solutions in the 15% of the variance accounted for by **Financial Capital.**

In other words, **"Japan, Inc."** is vulnerable to the substance, the sequence and the support of **Freedom Functions.** In short, it has no clue as to the meaning of **Freedom.**

In turn, **"Japan, Inc."** attempts to drive the empowering **NCD Components** by **Innovative Positioning:**

- **Innovative MCD Positioning,**
  ↓
- **Market-driven OCD,**
  ↓
- **Input-driven HCD,**
  ↓
- **Operations-driven ICD,**
  ↓
- **Standards-driven mCD.**

Together, these **NCD Components** are inadequate to implementing the **Innovative MCD Positioning** and accomplishing the **Capitalist-driven Functions.** Japan is most vulnerable with its limited **ICD:** its operational models are inferior to the vectorial models that provide direction and focus to the U.S. — vectorial models such as the very **NCD** that we are detailing. Again, you get what you plan for! Japan planned for **Imitative-Innovation!** And it got it!

Finally, **The Generative Thinking Processes** are dominated by an **Action-Orientation:**

- **Relating to Build Consensus;**
- **Representing Systems' Images;**
- **Reasoning to Act.**

Together, **Action-Oriented Thinking Processes** produce **Action Images** that enable **The NCD Components** to achieve **The Capitalistic Functions.**

The implications for **The Freedom Functions** are profound:

- Elevate **Capitalism** to **Free Enterprise Economics!**

- Rehabilitate **Mixed Governance** with **True Representative Governance!**

- Remediate **Cultural Relating** with **Socio-centric Empathy Training** to displace the current **Ego-Centric Version of Sympathy!**

Accomplishing these improvements will empower **The Innovative-Driven NCD** to accomplish an elevated **Free Enterprise Mission.**

Innovative Commercializer Positioning

Ordinarily, **"Japan, Inc."** would have **"IC" Positioning;** e.g., **"Japan, IC."** However, since the emphasis of its positioning is **Commercializing,** the positioning is **"Ci"** (See Figure 27). As may be seen, the **"Ci" Positioning** nests the **Innovative Initiatives** in the **Commercializer Phase.**

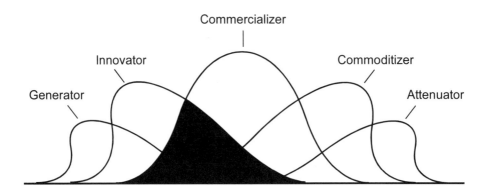

Figure 27. The Innovative Commercializer Phase

This is **"The Microsoft Model:"** to appear **"Slightly Innovative"** while becoming **Maximally Commercial.** The problem is that it may do neither. It is neither **Innovative** nor **Commercial** at the highest levels. Like Bill Gates, its people may end up walking around saying:

> *"The only thing that we fear is two guys in a garage who may change the game entirely."*

In other words, this apparently *"non-risk"* course is very vulnerable to **Generators** and **Innovators** as when the U.S. retaliated for *"dumping"* in the 1980s by pitting **True Innovation Versus Imitative-Innovation.**

To sum, **"Japan, Ci"** is still the second greatest **Commercializer** in the world with a **GDP** of over $5.5 trillion and **Per Capita Earnings** of over $43,000, not counting the 30,000 unemployed people who commit suicide each year. This amounts to one-half of U.S.A.'s $11 trillion **GDP** and eclipses the U.S.'s $32,000 **Per Capita.**

However, **"Japan, Ci"** never fully committed to becoming **The Innovator Nation. Innovation** is neither accomplished by the rote memorizations in its classrooms nor by the consensus-building in its corporations: **"Deska?"** (Translation: **"Is it not so?"**)

In transition, **"Japan, Ci"** has a great deal going for it. However, it is not an **Innovator-driven,** let alone a **Generator-driven Commercializer;** e.g., to have the **"GIC" Relationships** that the U.S.A. had at its high points. It may never accomplish these ambitions. It may always be a **"Wannabe."** Unless…

Unless it profoundly understands the relationship between **Freedom** and **Prosperity!** Unless it transforms its **Ancient and Mystical Culture** to a **Truly Free and Relating One!** Unless it surrenders the absurdity of its tautological belief that **"Homogeneity is Superiority — Genetic Superiority!"** Either you believe it or you don't!

Until then, **"Japan, Inc."** will keep sending its scientists and technologists to America and, after years of collaborative effort, some few may even learn enough and risk enough to win an occasional **Nobel Prize** for *"team breakthroughs"* in one area or another!

Until **"Japan, Ci"** trades in its **Past for its Future!**

Until **"Japan, Ci"** becomes **"Japan, Ic"** instead of **"Japan, Inc.!"**

IV. THE FUTURE OF FREEDOM

7. The Freedom Processes

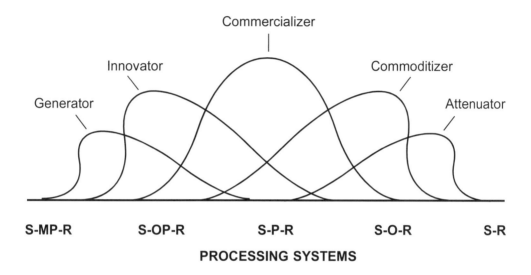

Commercializer

Innovator

Generator

Commoditizer

Attenuator

S-MP-R   **S-OP-R**   **S-P-R**   **S-O-R**   **S-R**

PROCESSING SYSTEMS

The socioeconomic issues and the geo-political crises of our time are a function of one overriding reason: the policymakers, architects and executives continue to function as conditioned, linear **Industrial Age** thinkers in the face of the spiraling and changing multidimensional and curvilinear **Information Age** complexity of their assignments. In other words, they are *"ignorant"* in the face of escalating complexity and, without **Generative Thinking Processes,** they are unable to reduce the problems to their **"Simplexity"** — just as we have reduced geo-political dimensions, political science, economy, sociology and psychology to the simple **Schematic** and **Spatial Representations.** Moreover, they are not ignorant because they are intellectually-challenged, but rather because, emotionally, they have chosen to remain culturally conditioned. **Intelligence is, after all, the ability to absorb one's environment, process its constructs, generate new initiatives, and grow by recycling feedback from experience!**

It is **all** about processing or thinking! The **S–R Conditioned** responding systems of **The Industrial Era** will simply not suffice for the **S–O–R Discriminative Learning** requirements of **The Information Age,** let alone **The S–P–R Generative Processing** requirements of **The Ideation Age** that is now upon us.

When the politicians, executives and bureaucrats say, *"We are sending our 'best and brightest'!"*, we may answer: *"From another age!"* The idea of returning to Classical Education is even more absurd than **"SOLs"** (Standards of Learning) for Public Education. At least, now we are testing for **S–R Systems;** under Classical Education, we would be testing for the **s–r Chained Expectancy Sequences** that undergird **S–R Conditioning.**

We can see the absurdity of **"Processing for the Past"** in Figure 28. The following may be noted:

- America was the sole **Market Generator!**
- There are no **True Market Innovators** — Japan is the only aspirant!
- All nations aspire to become **Market Commercializers!**

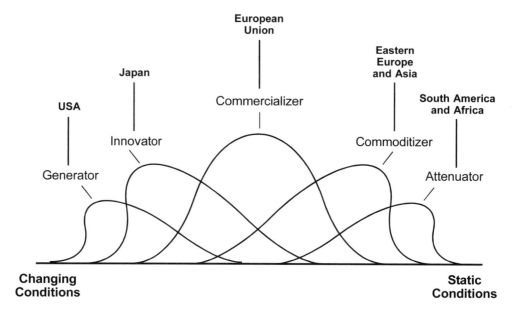

**Figure 28. An Illustration of Nations' Emphasis
Upon Market Phases**

Regarding America's **Generative–Innovator Leadership,** all
nations run in America's *"draft."* No other nations will dedicate
themselves to breaking their cultural learning and thinking molds, nor
take the entrepreneurial risks necessary to generate models to lead or
even contribute to the evolution and actualization of **The Global
Marketplace.**

Regarding the absence of **The Innovators,** the cost is still too high
and the profit too low for nations to dedicate themselves to bridging
the gap between **Generators** and **Commercializers.** In large part,
Innovation is a *"loss-leader"* and these nations do not go where their
financier *"angels"* fear to tread. Japan has carefully nested its
Innovative Initiatives in **The Commercializing Phase** as part of its
positioning to be **Slightly More Innovative** than its competitors.

Because of its **Human** and **Information Capital** derived from its **"Laboratory Industries,"** Israel is a candidate for becoming **Innovator** as it moves from **"The Last Bastion of Socialism"** to **Free Enterprise** by privatizing state assets and cutting the public sector, including entitlements to the ultra-Orthodox who refuse to work. However, taxed by survival efforts, Israel has not been able to clear the path for its **Brainpower** to focus upon **Market Breakthroughs and Transfers.** In this context, the **Arab-Israel** Crisis deserves an **Economic**—not a **Political Solution:** Israeli **Human Capital** empowering **Arab Human Resources** to become one of the world's most robust economies! (Relatedly, we have always worked to improve relations within antagonistic groups before bringing them together to relate between groups.)

From among **The Growing Commercializers,** nations such as Ireland are poised with the potential to become **Innovative Commercializers** due to their Economic Integration and Technological Connectivity. However, they are **I-Net-driven** by **"Best Practices"** and **"Best Ideas"** rather than **"Best Processes for Generating Best Ideas,"** e.g., **Generative Thinking Systems.**

From among the countries of the Mideast, the former British protectorates of Bahrain, Qatar and the United Arab Emirates are seeking to become **Commoditized Commercializers** by diversifying their energy-based economies. While gradually removing governmental burdens upon **Free Enterprise,** they lag behind in **"real"** relating and governance so that they are not too far **"out of line"** with their **Totalitarian** neighbors.

With the loss of Venezuela to **Totalitarianism,** South America has lost its exemplary performer for all of **The Freedom Functions.** While aspiring to leadership, recent reversals in spending restraints along with its **"sociogenetic cultural lag"** sentence Chile to the same **"quilombo"** or the environmental chaos of its Latin neighbors.

While all nations aspire to maximize profits in **The Commercializing Phase,** developing nations will settle transitionally for **Commoditizing** in which they produce more and more goods for less and less profit until, finally, they *"dump"* the goods and themselves in **Attenuating.** There are an infinite number of random ways to lose. There is only one model to win—substantively through **Human Brainpower** and **Free Enterprise.**

Indeed, most nations believe that **The Global Marketplace** is exclusively about profit-making commerciality. Wrong! If they continue to believe this after reading this work, they are not merely *"hard-wired"*—they are *"brain damaged."*

The Global Village and Its Marketplace are about accomplishing **The Freedom Functions:**

- **Interdependent Cultural Relating,**
- **Free Enterprise Economics,**
- **Free Democratic Governance.**

It is about empowering **The Possibilities Economy** so that we can actualize a **Truly Free Possibilities Civilization.**

Developmental Processing Systems

If we take another look at **The GICCA Curve,** we will see that developmental and cumulative processing systems undergird each phase (See Figure 29):

- **S–R Conditioned Responding** in **The Attenuating Phase;**

- **S–O–R Discriminative Learning** in **The Commoditizing Phase;**

- **S–P–R Generative Processing** in **The Commercializing Phase;**

- **S–OP–R Organizational Processing** in **The Innovating Phase;**

- **S–MP–R Marketplace Processing** in **The Generating Phase.**

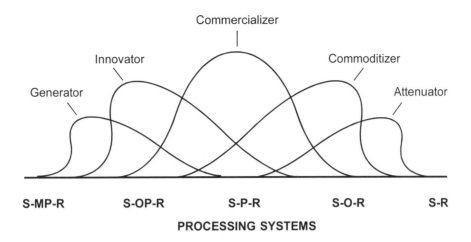

Figure 29. The Processing Systems of The GICCA Phases

- **S–R.** The **S–R Conditioned Responding** systems emphasize **"reflex"** responses (**R**) to conditioned stimuli (**S**). The **S–R** systems are always appropriate to the routinized requirements of automated and assembly-line jobs in **The Attenuation Phase.**

- **S–O–R.** The **S–O–R Discriminative Learning** systems emphasize the human organism's repository of **S–R** responses. This **S–O–R** repertoire enables the organism (**O**) to discriminate the stimulus conditions (**S**) and emit the appropriate response (**R**). The **S–O–R** systems are now appropriate to the elevating requirements for branching systems in the production of products and the delivery of services in **The Commoditizing Phase.**

- **S–P–R.** The **S–P–R Generative Processing Systems** emphasize the creation of new responses from the processor's repository of **S–O–R** responses. This **S–P–R** repertoire enables the processor (**P**) to represent the stimuli (**S**) and generate new and more powerful responses (**R**). The **S–P–R** systems are now appropriate for the elevating requirements to respond to the changing conditions of the stimulus environment in **The Commercializing Phase.**

- **S–OP–R.** The **S–OP–R** generative organizational processing systems emphasize the organization's creation of new responses from its repository of **S–P–R** responses. This **S–OP–R** repertoire enables the organizational processor (**OP**) to represent the organizational stimuli (**S**) and generate new and more powerful organizational responses (**R**). The **S–OP–R** systems are now appropriate for assembling new responses to meet the changing organizational conditions of **The Innovating Phase.**

- **S–MP–R.** The **S–MP–R** generative marketplace processing systems emphasize the leadership of organizations and communities in creating new positioning responses from their repository of **S–OP–R** responses. This **S–MP–R** repertoire enables the marketplace processor (**MP**) to discriminate the changing marketplace stimuli (**S**) and to generate more productive and profitable positioning responses (**R**). These **S–MP–R** systems are now required to generate continuously-changing positioning to meet the continuously-changing requirements of **The Generativity Phase.**

All processing requirements are elevating, indeed, escalating:

- Where **The Commoditizing Phase** once required **S–R** conditioning, it now requires **S–O–R** learning to assemble products or make service calls.

- Where **The Commercializing Phase** once required **S–O–R** discriminating, it now requires **S–P–R** thinking to generate new responses to changing customer **"DNA"** requirements.

- Where **The Innovating Phase** once required **S–P–R** individual processing, it now requires **S–OP–R** organizational processing to generate new responses to changing organizational **"DNA"** requirements.

- Where **The Generating Phase** once required **S–OP–R** organizational processing, it now requires **S–MP–R** marketplace processing to generate new positioning responses to meet the changing marketplace **"DNA"** requirements.

To sum, the conditions are continuously changing and, with them, the processing requirements are continuously elevating.

Clearly, the processing requirements are escalating. The reason The Third World is taking over the **Attenuating** jobs, within even **Commoditizing** and **Commercializing** is because the jobs require only **S–R Conditioned Responses.** These are appropriate steps in their learning curves!

The reason the so-called First and Second Worlds are unable to assume **Generating** and **Innovating** functions is because these positions require processing systems beyond their capabilities. There is no learning curve! No working curve! Only the damn brain damage of repetitious work to which our conditioned, linear-thinking leaders have led us.

Again, we may view the nested processing systems in Figure 30:

- **S–R Conditioned Responding Systems** and their **s–r Chaining Sub-Systems** condition responses for simple linear tasks in **The Industrial Age.**

- **S–O–R Discriminative Learning Systems** nest the **S–R Systems** and discriminate responses such as "Go–No Go" Branching Systems in **The Information Age.**

- **S–P–R Generative Processing Systems** nest the **S–O–R Systems** and generate new and improved responses for Multidimensional Systems in **The Ideation Age.**

- **S–OP–R Organizational Processing Systems** nest **S–P–R Systems** and generate new and more innovative organizational responses for the changing conditions of **The Age of Organization.**

- **S–MP–R Marketplace Processing Systems** nest **S–OP–R Systems** and generate new and more generative responses for the changing conditions of **The Age of Globalization.**

To sum, **The Developmental Processing Systems** undergird **The Phases of The GICCA Curve.**

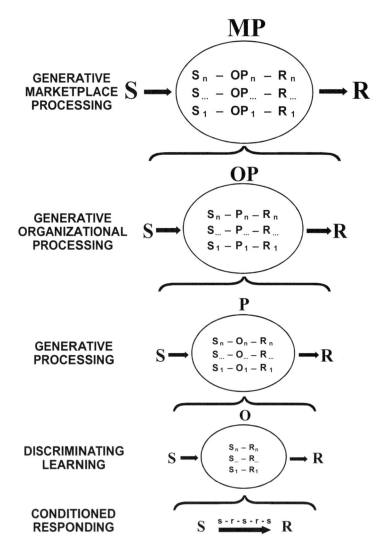

Figure 30. Developmental Processing Systems

The Developmental Processing Systems dictate **The Empowerment Stages** for embracing **The Global Marketplace:**

- **S–R** enables **Attenuating.**
- **S–O–R** enables **Commoditizing.**
- **S–P–R** enables **Commercializing.**
- **S–OP–R** enables **Innovating.**
- **S–MP–R** enables **Generating.**

At the highest levels of processing, **S–OP–R** enables **Innovative Transfers** into **The Changing Organization** while **S–MP–R** generates **Generative Breakthroughs** in the **Changing Marketplace.**

In summary, differential diagnosis dictates differential treatment:

- If diagnosed as a beginner, then we must conquer those precious **S–R Conditioning Systems** so we can contribute to the further **Attenuation** of **The Industrial Age.**

- If diagnosed at the **S–R** level, then we must consider learning **S–O–R Discriminative Learning Systems** so we can contribute to **Commoditizing** in the **Information Age.**

- If diagnosed at the **S–O–R** level, then we must consider learning **S–P–R Generative Processing Systems** so we can contribute to **Generating** in **The Age of Ideation.**

- If diagnosed at the **S–P–R** level (rare!), then we must consider learning **S–OP–R Organizational Processing Systems** so we can contribute to **Generating** in the **Age of Organization.**

- If diagnosed at the **S–OP–R** level (unheard of!), then we must consider learning **S–MP–R Marketplace Processing Systems** so we can contribute to **Generating** in the **Age of Globalization.**

- Finally, if diagnosed at the **S–MP–R** level, then you must join us or, better yet, mentor us in our search for the ingredients of **The Global Village and Its Marketplace.**

A special note about education is in order because of the critical nature of this resource. The advanced civilizations such as America have already skipped one revolution in learning: the **S–O–R Discriminative Learning Systems.** In order to prepare youth for the **Commercializing Marketplace** in the 21st century, these civilizations must now conquer and promulgate two revolutions in thinking: **S–O–R** and **S–P–R Generative Processing.**

Some expeditious recommendations follow:

1. **Train learners in thinking skills before "teaching" them any content.**

2. **Engage empowered learners in co-processing *all* content so that they can make the content instrumental for their purposes.**

The only thing that we can be sure of is that the content will change. So we are now empowering learners to process the changing content and, indeed, to contribute to its continuous change!

Regarding **Standards-of-Learning** or **SOL,** there are none! Simply stated, we cannot prescribe measurement of changing content. Here is what we can do to maintain **"Standards of Processing:"**

3. **Train teachers to operationally define all learning objectives (functions, components, processes, conditions, standards).**

That way they will know whether or when they have achieved their objectives.

Furthermore, teachers can expand **SOP** training to all parties with interests in the learning process:

4. **Train parents to operationally define learning objectives.**

That way the parents can both monitor teaching objectives as well as evaluate their own learning objectives.

Finally, we can culminate **SOP** by empowering the learners:

5. **Train learners to operationally define learning objectives.**

That way the learners can take charge of their own lifelong learning objectives in relation to their changing destinies.

In short, **there is no enduring content:** only ephemeral stimulus material to be processed by each succeeding generation. With each new wave of experience comes a new wave of **"generation."** Now we have given truly operational meaning to the term **"generation:"** it is not a linear and genetic inheritance; **it is a creative expression of ideation!**

In transition, **The Freedom Wars** are not political! They are not about the empty promises of security in **Totalitarian "take-overs." The Freedom Wars** are about processing and the substance it generates. They are about relating, empowering and freeing the exemplary performers in processing and, then, their followers. They are about processing to generate continually elevating levels of **Prosperity, Peace** and **Participation.** Either we care about future generations or we do not!

8. The Freedom Architecture

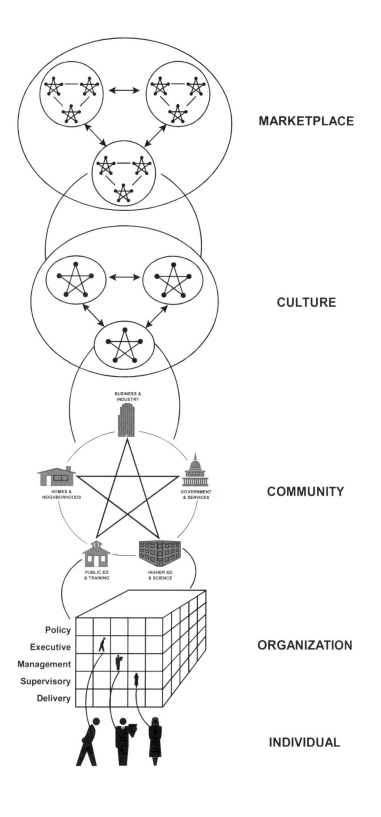

MARKETPLACE

CULTURE

BUSINESS &
INDUSTRY

HOMES &
NEIGHBORHOODS

GOVERNMENT
& SERVICES

COMMUNITY

PUBLIC ED
& TRAINING

HIGHER ED
& SCIENCE

Policy
Executive
Management
Supervisory
Delivery

ORGANIZATION

INDIVIDUAL

Clearly, Singapore is the exemplary model for a Third-World nation's entry into **The Global Marketplace.** Leaders like Lee and Goh designed an achievable mission for participating and, then, contributing to **The Growth Architecture** Collaborating with leading R & D centers, Singapore has thrived upon a state-architected entrepreneurial model.

Basically, it transferred the components of the internally-driven Japanese **"kieretsu"** to an externally-related Singaporean **"matrix."** The components were expanded to incorporate other nations, **Multinational Corporations** and leading research universities. The functions emphasized the changing commercial markets: from electronic and information technologies to pharmaceutical, biotechnological and now, nanotechnologies.

Since Singapore is itself a homogeneous and integrated community on a small island, it assumed community and cultural capital initiatives. The processes emphasized government-linked corporations or **GLCs** to pilot private sector organizational initiatives and state-mandated educational systems to prepare the human resources to manage these systems. What follows are preferred methodologies for generating capital marketplace initiatives: individual, organizational, community, cultural, marketplace.

The Freedom Architecture

The miraculous accomplishment of the **Information Technology (IT) Revolution** has been the **Internet** or **I-Net.** The I-Net has served to bring people together as never before; indeed, it has created **The Global Village.** This **Global Village** has served to invite people from everywhere — overriding all boundaries, national and otherwise — to participate in its **Global Marketplace.**

The **Global Marketplace** is a function of the trillions of decisions made in the marketplace every day. It communicates the decisions instantaneously, potentially making the information available to everyone who embraces it for purposes of their own decision-making. In so doing, it not only overrides national boundaries but also our historic concepts of economics — command and control, socialistic, even capitalistic — and serves to define a **Truly Free Enterprise Marketplace.**

The **Free Enterprise Market** also discounts the historic sources of economics, the natural resources that dominated the **Agrarian Age** and the machinery that sourced the **Industrial Age. Human Brainpower** becomes the generative source of the **Information Capital** that drives these grand new **Information** and **Ideation Ages.** The link between brainpower and the marketplace is **Entrepreneurial Initiative,** e.g., the different levels of human initiative that take place at different levels of organization: individuals, organizations, communities, cultures and marketplaces.

We may view the **Global Village and Its Marketplace** in Figure 31. As may be noted, the levels of human organizations range from individual and organizational through community and cultural to marketplace. Again, it is the level of initiative at each of these levels that determines its success in performance. We may conceive of these initiatives as freedom initiatives.

Individual Freedom

The largest journey begins with the smallest steps. The level of **Individual Freedom** is defined by **Individual Processing Systems** (See again Figure 31).[*] The **Generative Thinking Systems** are the foundation for all levels of human initiative:

- **Relating Systems** to share images of information and to negotiate new and personalized images;

---

[*] R. R. Carkhuff and D. Benoit. *The New 3Rs of Thinking: Possibilities Thinking and Individual Freedom.* HRD Press, 2004.

8. The Freedom Architecture

- **Representing Systems** to represent images of information at increasingly complex and multidimensional levels;

- **Reasoning Systems** to reason with representations of information to generate new and differentiated levels of initiative.

These **Generative Thinking Systems** are developmental and cumulative: reasoning is contingent upon the representing that is, in turn, dependent upon relating. The **Generative Thinking Systems** may be summarized as *"The New 3Rs of Thinking"* or *"Possibilities Thinking Systems."*

Dr. John Linder has demonstrated **Individual Freedom,** working with many groups of people in both academic and inner-city Philadelphia settings. He uses **"The New 3Rs"** as empowering skills for all **Individual Freedom.** First, he teaches the thinking skills. Next, he presents the topical areas that the people are addressing. The thinking skills enable **all** participants to generate new and more productive individual initiatives, initiatives that are instrumental for individual purposes. Having expanded the pool of possible initiatives, the groups can now focus upon selecting or generating the most powerful initiatives.

In this manner, **Possibilities Thinking** generates new and higher levels of initiative: intrapreneurial, entrepreneurial, extrapreneurial. In other words, **Individual Freedom** is a function of **Possibilities Thinking.**

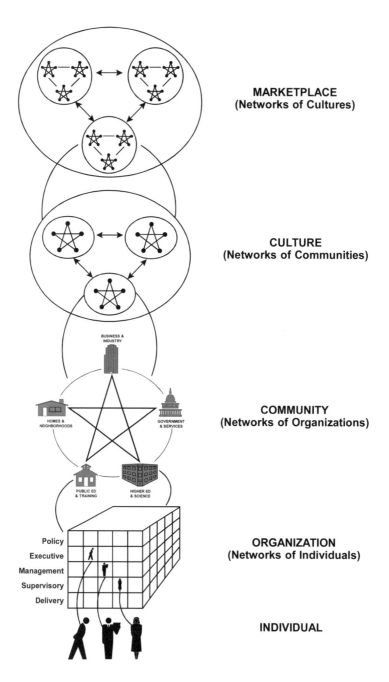

Figure 31. The Global Village and Marketplace

Organizational Freedom

The level of **Organizational Freedom** is defined by **Organizational Processing Systems.**[*] We define organizations as networks of individuals (See again Figure 31). When individuals are brought together in networks, they are dedicated to organizational initiatives. In order to generate these organizational initiatives, the individuals must employ their generative processing systems to process **The New Capital Development** functions of the organization:

- MCD or **Marketplace Positioning,**
- OCD or **Organizational Alignment,**
- HCD or **Human Processing,**
- ICD or **Information Modeling,**
- mCD or **Mechanical Tooling.**

Together, these systems define **The New Capital Development** or **NCD** functions of the organization.

To achieve **Organizational Freedom,** Peter Rayson and his associates at Airbus designed models for **"mainstreaming" The NCD Processing Systems** throughout the business.[**] Beginning with the strategic decision-makers, they processed to position their corporation as **"The Innovative Aircraft Producer."** Continuing with the executives and managers, they processed innovatively to align corporate resources with the positioning. Culminating with the human resources, they processed to innovate organizational alignment. They were successful at all levels of organizational functions in elevating **Organizational Freedom.**

In this manner, **The NCD Systems** empower the various organizational processors to generate images of information that incorporate individual initiative dedicated to powerful organizational initiatives.

---

[*] R. R. Carkhuff and B. G. Berenson. *The Possibilities Organization.* HRD Press, 2000.

[**] R. R. Carkhuff, et al. *The Possibilities Economy.* HRD Press, 2004.

They also prepare the various organizations to process interdependently within the community to generate powerful community initiatives. **Organizational Freedom** is demonstrated by each organization's generative initiatives—making decisions as to its own goals and aligning its resources to reach these goals.

Community Freedom

The level of **Community Freedom** is defined by **Community Processing Systems.**[*] Just as we define organizations as networks of individuals, so do we define communities as networks of organizations (See again Figure 31). When organizations are brought together developmentally and cumulatively, they are dedicated to community initiatives:

- **Homes and neighborhoods,** including churches, that emphasize basic **S–R Living Skills** such as relating skills and mechanical proficiencies that define basic **Mechanical Capital;**

- **Schools and training programs** that emphasize basic **S–O–R Learning Skills** such as **Learning-to-Learn** along with the knowledge acquired and the images developed as basic **Information Capital;**

- **Higher education and science and technology** that emphasize the **Generative S–P–R Thinking Skills** that define **Human Capital** at the highest levels;

- **Governance and its services** that emphasize the **S–OP–R Organizational Processing Systems** that deliver services and define **Organizational Capital** at the highest levels;

---

[*] R. R. Carkhuff, et al. *The Possibilities Community.* HRD Press, 2003.

8. The Freedom Architecture

- **Business and industry** that emphasize **S–MP–R Marketplace Processing Systems that position communities and businesses powerfully** to produce products and services and define **Marketplace Capital** at the highest levels.

Again, the community is organized developmentally and cumulatively from basic living to marketplace positioning.

The senior authors developed and implemented designs for **Community Freedom** in Springfield, Massachusetts. Basically, they designed a **"womb to tomb"** empowerment program to develop the community's level of **New Capital:**

- **MCD** or **Marketplace Capital Development** based upon community positioning for **Comparative Advantage** in the **Information Technology** marketplace;

- **OCD** or **Organizational Capital Development** aligning all organizational resources with community positioning;

- **HCD** or **Human Capital Development** based upon empowerment in human processing skills dedicated to organizational alignment;

- **ICD** or **Information Capital Development** based upon empowerment in information modeling to implement human processing;

- **mCD** or **Mechanical Capital Development** based upon empowerment in mechanical tooling to implement information modeling.

Again, the **NCD** systems are developmental and cumulative in the community organizations: homes and neighborhoods, schools and training, higher education, governance and services, business and industry. This means that building upon the most immature form of **NCD,** the different community organizations dedicate their **Generative Thinking Systems** to higher-order **NCD: ICD, HCD, OCD, MCD. Community Freedom** is demonstrated by community initiatives to empower and align **NCD** in the community.

Cultural Freedom

The level of **Cultural Initiative** is defined by **Cultural Processing Systems.**[*] Just as we defined communities as networks of organizations, now we define cultures as networks of communities (See again Figure 31). When communities are brought together, they are dedicated to cultural initiatives:

- **Cultural relating to become participants in the Global Marketplace;**

- **Free enterprise economics to generate wealth in the Global Marketplace;**

- **Direct democratic governance to empower wealth-generation in the Global Marketplace.**

Together, we label these initiatives **The Freedom Functions.**

Dr. Andrew Griffin has established **"Cultural Freedom Groups"** in his **"Ethnic Think Tanks."** Comprised of First American, Asian American, Black American, Hispanic American and marginal Anglo American membership, these **"Freedom Groups"** have concentrated upon the following **Freedom Functions:**

- **Interdependent Cultural Relating** within, between, and among ethnic groups, culminating in educational community and cultural initiatives;

- **Entrepreneurial-driven Free Enterprise,** culminating in new business enterprise;

- **Direct Democratic Governance,** culminating in legislation requiring strategic input from any group impacted by legislation.

---

[*] R. R. Carkhuff, et al. *The Possibilities Culture.* HRD Press, 2003.

In short, the **Generative Thinking Systems** are dedicated to the **NCD** necessary to empower achievement of **The Freedom Functions** at the highest levels: **Cultural Relating, Free Enterprise, Direct Democracy. Cultural Freedom** is demonstrated by the cultural initiatives of networks of communities to enable achievement of **The Freedom Functions.**

Marketplace Freedom

The level of **Marketplace Freedom** is defined by **Marketplace Processing Systems.**[*] Once again, the marketplace is a network of cultures that come together to define their differences, market their wares, and process their benefits (See again Figure 31). When cultures are brought together in this manner, they are dedicated to marketplace initiatives:

- **Cultural relating to differentiate,**
- **Free enterprise to generate,**
- **Direct democracy to participate.**

Together, **The Freedom Functions** define our networking in the global marketplace.

Dr. Griffin has culminated his **"Ethnic Think Tanks"** by converging for one common purpose: To accomplish **The Freedom Functions** that will project them into **The Global Marketplace:**

- To relate culturally at the highest levels of collaboration culminating in interdependent processing;

- To initiate economically at the highest levels of capitalism, culminating in entrepreneurial free enterprise;

- To initiate governmentally at the highest levels of participation, culminating in direct democratic governance.

---

[*] R. R. Carkhuff, et al. *The GICCA Curve: The Possibilities Marketplace.* HRD Press, 2004.

To this end, he, himself, has related, empowered and freed the American Indians, Asians, Blacks, Hispanics, and marginal Whites to converge upon marketplace initiatives.

Once again, Singapore has been our exemplar for marketplace initiative. **Marketplace Freedom** is demonstrated by the marketplace initiatives of a network of cultures. These networks of cultures participate to govern their relationships peacefully, generate new products and services for economic prosperity, and differentiate their unique cultural perspectives to promote the advancement of civilization. **Marketplace Freedom** or **Global Freedom** enables freedom for cultures, communities, organizations and individuals.

In summary, **The Architecture of Freedom** is a nested vision of initiatives. At its core is **Individual Freedom.** Organizations are nested in communities, communities in cultures, and cultures in the marketplace. Together these are the contexts or conditions under which individual freedom will either emerge or be strangled. It is incumbent upon each of us to initiate to free ourselves and ultimately to free all of humanity, for we are all interdependently related.

V. FREEDOM AND CHANGEABILITY

9. The Freedom-Building Technologies

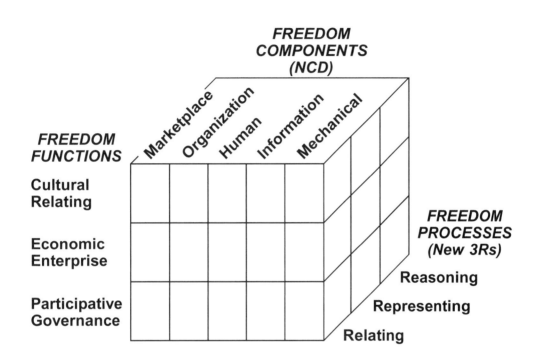

All **Freedoms** begin with **Individual Freedom.** All **Individual Freedom** begins with **Thinking** culminating in **Initiative.** The following is an autobiographical history beginning with **Individual Freedom** leading to all forms of **Freedom — Organizational, Community, Cultural, Marketplace.**

Andrew H. Griffin, Jr. was a poor black boy, born in the inner city of Springfield, Massachusetts, the sixth oldest of seventeen children. His father worked two jobs to support his family, and his mother spent long days providing the physical and psychological nourishment to a family that now includes more than 70 grandchildren. Andy, as he is now known to his professional colleagues, will always be "Bootsie" to the family from whom he has both drawn and given responsive strength and initiative support. Here is how he sees the development of his maturity.

Individual Freedom

I come from a family of seventeen and never thought of being poor until I went to college and they talked about poverty levels according to income and number of people in a family. I was taught to believe that no one was better than I. Nor I better than anyone else. My parents taught us to recognize opportunity and that everyone should be given the same opportunity. They encouraged us to be individuals but demanded that we do our best, as well as be able to accept the consequences for whatever we did. My mother tended to be understanding. My father tended to be demanding. They complemented each other. Both my mother and father were very, very strong and had a 360-degree reinforcement program in all the areas. They loved and fought violently. It was an "either-or" world. You did or you didn't. It was very easy for me to understand that. They accepted all people, regardless of race, and allowed us to join or participate in all constructive activities. My sisters could play baseball and basketball equal to my brothers and myself. The idea of sexism was foreign to me. Although I recognized the difference in color, it was really the capabilities of a person that made a real difference.

As I grew up, my mother and father sat "upon my shoulders" many times when I was about to make a major decision. More often than not, my behavior was influenced by what I thought they would have done. It is still from this background I draw much of my thinking, regardless of what the research or renowned people say. My early experiences in life with my mother and father provided me with the foundation for later life. Whatever I did, whether I felt comfortable or not, they were concerned that I did it with the best of my energies. Because my mother was able to remain at home, I knew that I was able to reach her at any time. Psychologically and realistically this provided me with a genuine support system. My father constantly assessed and challenged me in all the activities that I became a part of, including leading demonstrations that he did not fully appreciate.

I also learned a lot of life's lessons in playing ball. Most of all, I learned not to place limits on my performance. I found I could do a lot of things that I did not think possible. I learned to do things better and better. I transferred these learnings to the classroom and learned to achieve in school.

*The first set of **Freedom-Building** skills that I learned was **Individual Thinking:***

- ***Exploring** by analyzing my experience,*
- ***Understanding** by synthesizing my objectives,*
- ***Acting** by operationalizing my programs.*

*These skills empowered me to generate individual initiatives and, thus, my own **Individual Freedom.** I was ready to dedicate my individual thinking to larger purposes.*

Organizational Freedom

I always knew that there was a limit to what individuals could accomplish by themselves. I was oriented to participating, contributing and finally leading in organizations. I viewed organizations like the teams that I played on:

- *The military where I rose to sergeant in the U.S. Marines;*

- *Football, where I rose to the professional level with the Green Bay Packers;*

- *College, where I rose to the doctoral level with a Harvard degree.*

*However, what really facilitated the explosion of my growth was participating as co-director and then director of the Center for Human Resource Development at a small college, American International College, in the middle of a black ghetto. This organization was dedicated to the mission of Human Resource Development, or HRD. The second set of **Freedom-Building** skills that I learned was **Organizational Processing Systems.** We all worked interdependently to develop all organizational functions:*

- *Policy-making for positioning ourselves to relate to people and human resources;*

- *Executive architecture to develop skills programs and curricula to empower people;*

- *Management systems to manage skills development programs for community people, undergraduates and graduate students;*

- *Supervisory processes to achieve skills objectives in all areas of HRD;*

- *Delivery programs to implement the tasks to achieve the HRD objectives.*

Above all else, I learned to think – individually and interpersonally:

- *Getting others' images of things;*
- *Giving my images of things;*
- *Merging our mutual images of things.*

*With this backdrop, I adopted the theme: **"Ain't no stoppin' us now!"***
*Our organizational units were focused interdependently: **"Mutual processing for mutual objectives."***

Community

*We emphasized the community as a **"network of organizations."** These skills empowered us to generate organizational initiatives and, thus, achieve our **Organizational Freedom.***

We focused upon the community by viewing all other entities in the community:

- *Homes, neighborhoods and churches,*
- *Schools and training programs,*
- *Higher education and technology,*
- *Government and its services,*
- *Business and industry.*

*The third set of **Freedom-Building** skills that I learned was **Community Processing Systems:** We related to all of these entities interdependently.*

- *To develop parenting and early childhood programs as well as **"Head-Start"** programs for basic **"learning-to-learn"** needs;*

- *To develop educational and tutorial programs to accelerate the development of skills in conventional education systems and **"New Careers"** programs for people with non-conventional needs;*

- *To develop higher education and technologies for advanced training programs in higher-order generative processing systems;*

- *To elevate governance and service programs in the basic needs of housing, welfare, justice and recreation systems;*

- *To elevate business and industry's community involvement by engaging them in enlightened policy-making with community leaders while supplying them with improved human capital for their work requirements.*

*In short, we assumed leadership in initiating and coordinating programs **"from womb to tomb."** These skills empowered us to generate community initiatives and, thus, achieve our **Community Freedom.***

Culture

Most of my life, I thought of community as the highest order of organization. As I mentioned, I understood that culture itself was no more – nor less – than a **"network of communities"** *and what they believe about themselves.*

I began working with different cultures in what we labeled **"Ethnic Think Tanks:"**

- *Black cultures,*
- *White cultures,*
- *Hispanic cultures,*
- *Asian cultures*
- *Island cultures*

Each of these cultures conceived of themselves in terms of their uniqueness. Each discovered their commonalities: They were indeed **"communities of communities."**

In this context, I discovered my fourth set of **Freedom-Building** *skills to be* **"Cultural Processing Systems:"**

- *"How did the cultures want to relate to other cultures?"*
- *"How would they support these relationships economically?"*
- *"How would they support these relationships governmentally?"*

The answers we discovered were truly rational.

Most everyone wanted to relate independently with other cultures (without understanding that relating and independence constitute an oxymoron or a conflict in meaning).

Most everyone realized that they need to commit to some form or another of capitalistic economics in order to accomplish this independence.

Most everyone recognized that they required supportive representative governance to implement the capitalism and accomplish the independence mission.

With each cultural grouping, we were able to summarize the functions to which free cultures aspire:

- ***Cultural Relating,***
- ***Free Enterprise Economics,***
- ***Free and Direct Democratic Governance.***

*We label these **"The Freedom Functions".** We dedicate our cultures to achieving them. These skills empowered us to generate cultural initiatives and, thus, achieve our **Cultural Freedom.***

Marketplace

*It has been in my maturity that I began to understand the role of cultures in defining the marketplace: **"The marketplace is a network of cultures."** My fifth set of **Freedom-Building** skills was **"Marketplace Processing Systems."***

I began working with different cultures to define the marketplace for their contributions. Working with the leaders of each culture, we established training cadres for exporting our learnings and skills to other cultures.

*Again, in meeting with other cultures, we defined each other in terms of **"The Freedom Functions."** Most often, we found that these newly-addressed cultures were functioning at low levels:*

- ***Dependent Cultural Relating,***
- ***Controlled Economics,***
- ***Totalitarian Governance.***

*We worked with them to elevate both their perspectives and their performance on **"The Freedom Functions."** These skills empowered us to generate marketplace initiatives and, thus, achieve our **Marketplace Freedom.***

Together, the skills programs that we designed ran parallel to the experiences that I have detailed:

- *Individual initiative leading to **Individual Freedom;***
- *Organizational initiative leading to **Organizational Freedom;***
- *Community initiative leading to **Community Freedom;***
- *Cultural initiative leading to **Cultural Freedom;***
- *Marketplace initiative leading to **Marketplace Freedom.***

*In all instances, we empowered the cultures in the skills that they required to participate in **"The Global Village and Its Marketplace."***

*We labeled the **Freedom-Building** projects, **"The Seed of Freedom"**, and deliver them to you now. It all begins with **Individual Freedom.***

Before initiating **Freedom-Building Programs,** we must refer to the models we are employing.

The **Freedom Model** may be viewed in its totality in Figure 32. As may be noted, **The Freedom Functions** are accomplished by **New Capital Development** or **NCD Components** enabled by **Generative Thinking Processes** or **The New 3Rs Processes:**

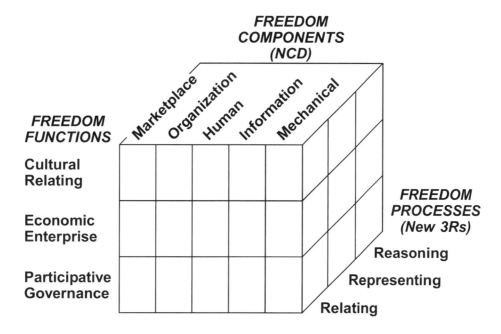

Figure 32. The Freedom Model

This means that we accomplish our **Freedom Functions** by **New Capital Development** enabled by **Generative Thinking Systems.** In short, we need to think initiatively in order to participate entrepreneurially in accomplishing **The Freedom Functions.**

In short, there is a **Model for Initiating in the Global Marketplace** — to participate, to contribute, to lead. It remains for us to make intentional and, indeed, initiative decisions to do so. What follow are the **Empowerment Programs** for individual, organizational, community, cultural and marketplace initiatives for achieving **Freedom.**

Phase I — Empowering Individual Initiatives

Goal: To empower individual initiative by training in **The New 3Rs of Thinking Skills** (See Figure 33).

Objectives: The New 3Rs of Thinking

- R^1 — **Relating skills** that enable individuals to relate productively by getting, giving, and merging information;
- R^2 — **Representing skills** that enable individuals to represent information productively in sentences, systems and scales;
- R^3 — **Reasoning skills** that enable individuals to reason with information powerfully by exploring, understanding and acting initiatively upon the information.

Benefits: New 3Rs → **Individual Initiatives**

- **Living Functions** such as home and family;
- **Learning Functions** such as education and training;
- **Working Functions** such as performance and production.

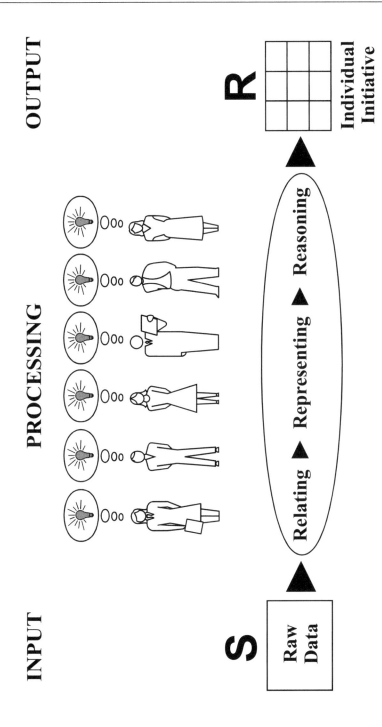

Figure 33. Empowering Individual Freedom

Phase II — Empowering Organizational Initiatives

Goal: To empower organizations to make community initiatives **"I"** by acquiring and applying **The New Capital Development Systems** (See Figure 34).

Objectives: The New Capital Development Systems

- **MCD — Marketplace Capital Development** or positioning in the marketplace;
- **OCD — Organizational Capital Development** or aligning organization resources with positioning;
- **HCD — Human Capital Development** or human processing to implement organization alignment;
- **ICD — Information Capital Development** or information modeling to implement human processing;
- **mCD — Mechanical Capital Development** or mechanical tooling to implement information modeling.

Benefits: New 3Rs x NCD → Organizational Initiatives

- **Policy Functions** such as **missioning;**
- **Executive Functions** such as **organizing;**
- **Management Functions** such as **systematizing;**
- **Supervisory Functions** such as **operationalizing;**
- **Delivery Functions** such as **technologizing.**

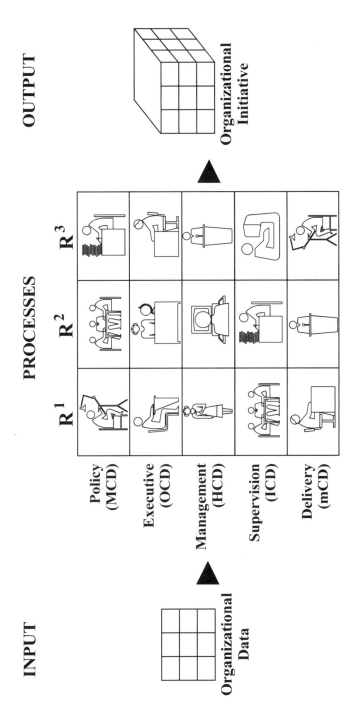

OUTPUT

Organizational
Initiative

PROCESSES

R³

R²

R¹

INPUT

Organizational
Data

Policy
(MCD)

Executive
(OCD)

Management
(HCD)

Supervision
(ICD)

Delivery
(mCD)

Figure 34. Empowering Organizational Freedom

Phase III — Empowering Community Initiatives

Goal: To empower organizations to make community initiatives "I" by acquiring and applying **The New Capital Development Systems** (See Figure 35).

Objectives: **Community Capital Development Systems**

- **Homes and Neighborhoods** emphasizing **mCD;**
- **Education and Training** emphasizing **mCD** and **ICD;**
- **Higher Education** emphasizing **mCD, ICD** and **HCD;**
- **Governance** emphasizing **mCD, ICD, HCD** and **OCD;**
- **Business** emphasizing **mCD, ICD, HCD, OCD** and **MCD.**

Benefits: New 3Rs x NCD → **Community Initiatives**

- **Home Functions** to prepare people to **relate** to information
- **School Functions** to empower learners to **represent** information;
- **College Functions** to empower thinkers to **reason** with information;
- **Governance Functions** to empower organizations to process community information and **align resources;**
- **Business Functions** to empower corporations to process marketing information and **position community.**

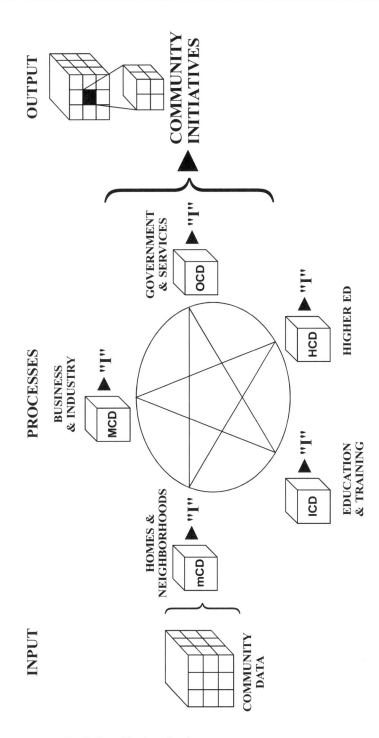

Figure 35. Empowering Community Freedom

Phase IV — Empowering Cultural Initiatives

Goal: To empower communities to make cultural initiatives by acquiring and applying **The Freedom Functions** (See Figure 36).

Objectives: **The Freedom Functions (FF)**

- **Cultural Relating** to initiate collaboratively with other communities;
- **Free Enterprise** to initiate entrepreneurially in economics with other communities;
- **Participative Governance** to initiate directly in governance with other communities.

Benefits: New 3Rs x NCD x Freedom Functions (FF) → Cultural Initiatives

- **Initiative thinking** in **individuals;**
- **Individual integration** in **organizations;**
- **Organizational integration** in **communities;**
- **Community integration** in **cultures;**
- **Cultural integration** in **marketplace.**

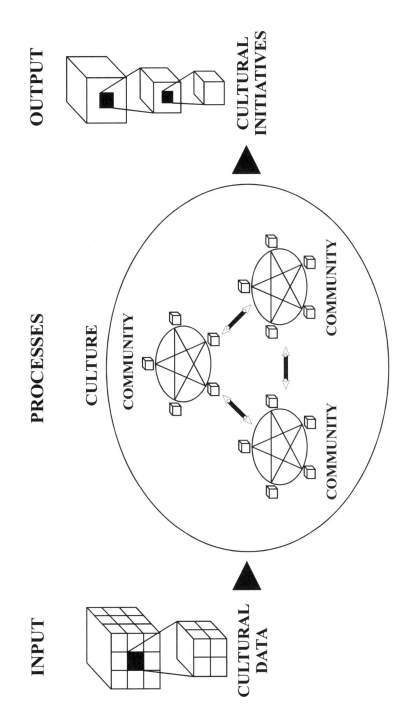

OUTPUT

CULTURAL INITIATIVES

PROCESSES

CULTURE

COMMUNITY

COMMUNITY

COMMUNITY

COMMUNITY

INPUT

CULTURAL DATA

Figure 36. Empowering Cultural Freedom

Phase V — Empowering Marketplace Initiatives

Goal: To empower cultures to make marketplace initiatives by acquiring and applying **The Freedom Doctrine Design** (See Figure 37).

Objectives: The Freedom Doctrine Systems

- **Freedom Functions (FF)**
- **New Capital Development (NCD) Components**
- **The New 3Rs Processes**

Benefits: Freedom Doctrine → Marketplace Initiatives

- **New 3Rs → Individual Initiative**
- **New 3Rs x NCD → Organizational Initiative**
- **New 3Rs x NCD → Community Initiative**
- **New 3Rs x NCD x FF → Cultural Initiative**
- **Freedom Doctrine → Marketplace Initiative**

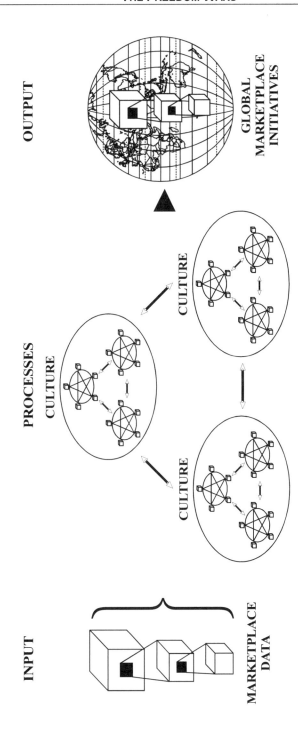

OUTPUT

GLOBAL MARKETPLACE INITIATIVES

PROCESSES

CULTURE

CULTURE

CULTURE

INPUT

MARKETPLACE DATA

Figure 37. Empowering Marketplace Freedom

9. The Freedom-Building Technologies

In summary, the mission of **Freedom-Building** may be viewed in **The Freedom Model** (See again Figure 37): To develop **The Architecture for Global Freedom.** This architecture culminates in **The Global Village and Its Marketplace:**

I. Empowering **Individual Initiatives** by training in **The New 3Rs Thinking Skills;**

II. Empowering **Organizational Initiatives** by dedicating **The New 3Rs** to organizational functions;

III. Empowering **Community Initiatives** by training in **The New Capital Development Systems;**

IV. Empowering **Cultural Initiatives** by training in **The Freedom Functions;**

V. Empowering **Marketplace Initiatives** by relating **The Cultural Systems.**

The **Marketplace Initiatives** culminate in the first model for **The Global Village and Its Marketplace.** Indeed, the **Freedom-Building Websites** will provide the first demonstrable and measurable indices of the existence of **The Global Village and Its Marketplace.**

In summary, the facts of its existence are worth reviewing:

- **The Internet and other Information Age phenomena have created a Global Village and Its Marketplace.**

- **The Global Marketplace has shifted the source of socioeconomic growth to Human Brainpower and the NCD that it generates in The New Age of Ideation.**

- **Our Human Brainpower has shifted the emphasis to Human Processing as the source of initiative — intrapreneurial, entrepreneurial, extrapreneurial.**

In transition, it is the very **Individualism** that has characterized the American experience that the world needs to emulate and — dare we say — imitate. For we are now made in the image of a **Global Village.**

Individualism and **Global Freedom!** One is not possible without the other!

10. The Freedom Culture

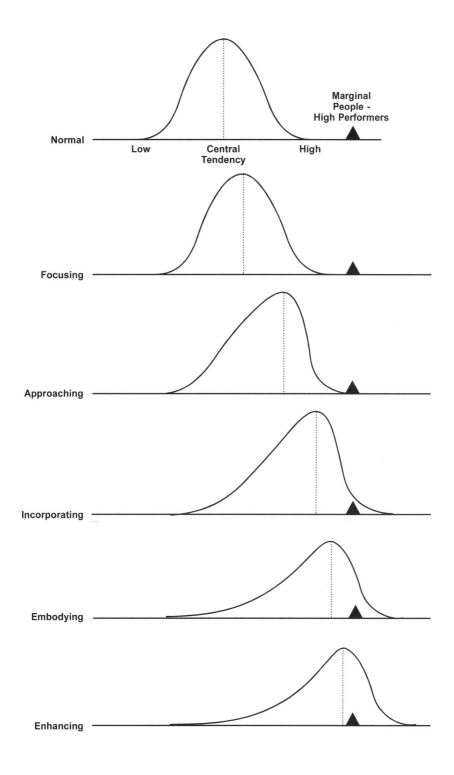

Normal   Low   Central   High
Tendency

Marginal
People -
High Performers

Focusing

Approaching

Incorporating

Embodying

Enhancing

The differences between **Freedom** and **Totalitarianism** may be heard in the tale of the peasant who, upon his way to work, discovers a genie in a bottle. Having escaped the bottle, the genie inquires as to the peasant's *"one wish."* The peasant replies:

> *"I have eight cows and my neighbor has 16. I'd like you to kill eight of his."*

Historically, culture has been viewed as groupings of people by racial, ethnic and national characteristics. Assumedly, without an understanding of cultural heritage, the economic and social endeavors of these people might not be understood. In this context, then, culture extends to give meaning to the economic and social as well as the esthetic and intellectual character of peoples.

Inherent in the assumptions of culture is the principle that culture is defined by past traditions. In point of fact, no matter how beautiful the music, art and literature, culture is defined by conditioned responding systems appropriate to the requirements of the conditions under the **Totalitarian Systems** of their times.

The Future of Freedom

Somewhere at the end of the 20th century, a new definition of culture evolved. In this definition, culture is defined futuristically by the evolving requirements of **The Global Village and Its Marketplace.** This is the **Generative Definition of Culture.** This definition does not exclude traditional values. Rather, like the enlightened individual making a critical decision, the person employs **The Freedom Matrix** to relate values to requirements in an attempt to maximize both.

The Freedom Wars began with the emergence of America and its evolving **Freedom Systems:**

- **States that related collaboratively and peacefully,**
- **States that generated extraordinary wealth,**
- **States that were governed by their policy-making citizens.**

Together, these states converged to generate the most free and collaboratively relating, enterprising and governing system in the history of humankind, the U.S.A. In so doing, the U.S. defined **The Freedom Systems** in the futuristic terms of **Cultural Relating, Free Enterprise** and **Participative Governance.**

Simultaneously, the **Totalitarian Cultures** of the world have risen up to attack and, now, terrorize the **Freedom Systems.** Having flunked **The 20th Century Tests of Totalitarianism,** leaving 150 million dead behind their empty promises and deathly weaponry, these **Totalitarian Cultures** now seek to slow-down, weigh-down, batter-down the **Freedom System in The 21st Century.**

Universally, these **Totalitarian** peoples and nations seek to hold on to their **Dysfunctional Cultures.** Uniformly, they have agreed upon one common solution:

> *Steal the* **"Secrets"** *of Freedom while maintaining the Totalitarianism of their cultures!*

They do not comprehend that the **"Secrets" of Freedom** are not at all secrets. They do not understand that the **"Public Principles of Freedom"** are antithetical to everything their **Totalitarian Cultures** dictate and tolerate.

Totalitarianism and Variability

We can understand the evolution of cultures best with a comparison of the **Destruct System** of **Totalitarianism** with the **Construct System** of **Freedom:**[*]

The central tendency in an **Unfree Society** becomes institutionalized (See Figure 38). The first stage of **The Destruct System** may be conceived of as an **Ignorance Stage,** and ignorance is always intentional. As can be seen, the logical goal of facilitating peoples' or culture's development toward a higher level of functioning is ignored. This situation occurs when those in the mainstream treat high functioning people just as they treat low functioning people. It is just too much work for the comfortable people to become productive people. At most, they need energy to adapt to their circumstances; they are caught up in an incentive system that demands very little and rewards them handsomely; they care not about the people around them; they get away with vague concepts of efforts at work; they involve themselves only in the minimum learning necessary to insure their comfort; they are concerned only with being critics, diagnosing others from an external frame of reference. They seek to institutionalize these characteristics and make people over in their images. That way they will always be comfortable and never be vulnerable—even as they die, physically, emotionally, intellectually and spiritually.

---

[*] R. R. Carkhuff, *Toward Actualizing Human Potential.* Amherst, MA: 1981.

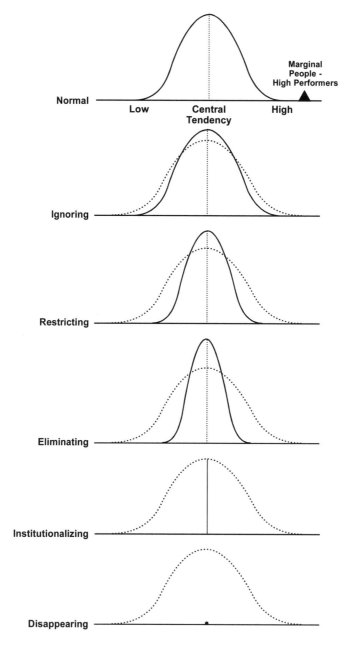

Figure 38. The Movement Toward Restricted
Variability of Unfree

What happens during the second stage of **The Destruct System,** a **Stage of Restriction,** is that the variability becomes more and more restricted. This is accomplished by channeling the extremes on any index into the mainstream. Thus, the highs and the lows become fewer and less prominent and the central tendency is accentuated.

This restrictiveness is carried to an extreme of **"Leptokurticism"** during the third **Stage of Elimination.** During this stage, those marginal peoples—high and low—who were not **"mainstreamed"** for one reason or another are eliminated. Thus, the central tendency is further exaggerated as the peoples come increasingly to look like each other.

The fourth stage may be conceived of as a **Destructive Stage,** although the process has been destructive throughout. Finally, all variance is destroyed and encompassed within one single dimension on any one index. We see this most clearly in advanced stages of all authoritarian societies. The people are made over in the image of their leader or leaders.

The fifth **Stage of Institutionalization** may also be considered the **Disappearing Stage.** Since all peoples appear as one, they can be represented as one. Indeed, the one can be reduced until it has disappeared. The culmination of the institutionalization of humankind is the disappearance of humanity. We see this most clearly in the advanced stages of all totalitarian societies. The people are made over in the image or their leader or leaders. And their leaders are one-dimensional people with one principle of operating—either you are controlled or you are eliminated. In the end, such a system self-destructs.

Even when such a system is overthrown, as in a revolution from within or without, the stages are usually repeated: **One source of restrictive variance is replaced with another.** Surely, there is utility in doing this when a system is diseased. However, such a program kills or cures. It does not grow, because it maximizes intervention and control and abandons or eliminates sources of variance.

Freedom and Changeability

The central tendency in a **Free Society** becomes mobilized (See Figure 39). The first stage of **The Construct System** may be conceived of as a **Focusing Stage.** In a sense, the main body of the variance targets the cultures of marginal people. The people observe the success of the marginal peoples' operations. And if a significant number of its people—perhaps ten to twenty percent—are attracted to the success, they mobile to incorporate it.

During the second stage of **The Construct System,** the main body of variance begins to **Approach** the successful marginal people. The curve begins to be skewed in the direction of the marginal people as the society seeks to incorporate their healthful potency.

In the third stage, the society begins to **Incorporate** the successful marginal people. In the process of being skewed fully in the direction of the marginal people, there is a tendency for the tail in the other, less functional direction to diminish in size. Thus, people at the less functional end of the continuum are mobilized to move toward the main body of variance.

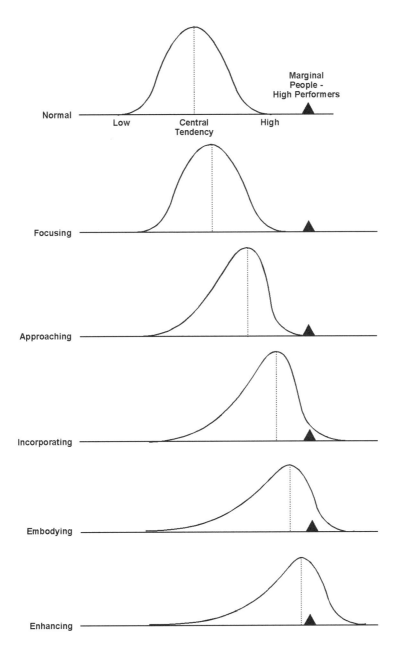

Figure 39. The Movement Toward Increasing Variability in Free Societies

In the fourth stage, the society begins to **Embody** the successful marginal people. In a sense, it has mainstreamed the successful attributes and made them the mode rather than the deviation. At the same time, it is eliminating more of the variance from the less functional end of the continuum.

Finally, in the last stage, the society actually seeks to **Enhance** the attributes of the successful marginal people. It models and, thus, represents what was once deviant. Also, whether inadvertently or not, it sets the stage for the new variations off the now **"mainstreamed theme."** Thus, by representing the attributes of the once-marginal person, society creates the conditions for the development of newly marginal people who will serve to move society still further in the direction of effectiveness.

In summary, **The Construct System** produces people who are more variable in a relative sense and more healthy in an absolute sense. A society dominated by such a system is always skewed toward the fully-functioning. person. Such a society is always creating variability by its expanding tolerance limits and its evolutionary growth disposition. Such a society is always moving toward effectiveness and, thus, toward health.

The Construct System is a **Changeability System.** Rather than to replace one restricted source of variance with another as in a revolutionary system, it adds variance in an evolutionary manner. It works effectively when there are healthy aspects of the system to be incorporated and these healthy aspects, in turn, evolve in a free society. It grows by minimizing intervention or control and maximizing variance. It maximizes existing sources of variance by adding incrementally without fundamental alterations.

In the beginning, people are in trouble because they have too few responses available to them. Along the way, fewer people are in difficulty because more people have larger repertoires of responses. In the end, such a system has extensive variability among people functioning at high levels of whatever index is employed.

Such a system is consistent with the laws of science and nature. It is organic in terms of utilizing its own resources as the sources of its own power. It is dynamic in terms of evolving constantly in more and more efficacious forms. It conserves energy in minimizing its investment and maximizing its return. It allows evolution to work at a maximum rate in maximizing the contribution of humans to humans.

The key to the development of a relatively more variable and absolutely more healthy society is the variability of fully functioning peoples or exemplars. Fully functioning people are, by definition, more variable on certain specialty dimensions than the society in which they exist. (Indeed, **Free Individuals** are infinitely more variable than **All Other Totalitarian Societies Summed Together!**) It is precisely this variability that makes it attractive for society to move toward fully functioning people to incorporate them. It is also this same variability that distinguishes fully functioning people from other marginal peoples who are dysfunctional but with whom totalitarian societies tend to confuse the fully functioning person.

In turn, the key to the fully functioning peoples' variability is their marginality—the ability to see things from a unique perspective; to see the subtle nuances of old dimensions; to develop the full richness of new dimensions. It is this marginality that enables the fully functioning people to actualize their potential and to give society the opportunity to actualize its potential.

For example, all of the movements with **"Human"** adjectives began in America with approaches to successful, marginal peoples: **Human Relations, Human Resources, Human Capital, Human Rights, Human Sciences.** This is seen in the **Great American Civil Rights Movement** that moved from **Physical Slavery** and **Intellectual Servitude** through **Ethical** and **Legal Mandates** toward **Fully-Functional,** if not **Morally Operational, Human Rights.** It has left the *"segregationists"* behind to expire at the tail of the moving curve only to encounter the *"elitists"* and the *"classists"* and the *"other-ists."* So what else is new? The movement continues toward the healthy people.

Another illustration is **Globalization.** As the nations move from **Dependency and Reactivity** through **Independence and Protectionism,** to **Interdependence and Reciprocity,** they encounter the same experiences: **Movement to incorporate the marginal peoples or the high performers.** Healthy civilizations require this movement, whatever the protestations of **"The Luddites."**

In conclusion, the healthiest societies are moving in the direction of the **Actualizers**—the once marginal peoples whom other societies sought to eliminate. **Actualizers** are the sources of creativity and productivity whom constructive societies seek to cultivate. Such societies are moving in the direction of their own **Self-Actualization.** Such a society is within our grasp (Carkhuff, 1981, pp. 139–144).

* * * * *

The Freedom Culture

The fact is that America does create **The Free Enterprise System.** Without its **Generativity,** there is no **Free Enterprise:**

- **No Innovation of the Breakthroughs!**
- **No Commercialization of the Transfers!**
- **No Commoditization of Commerciality!**

Just look again at the **GICCA Curve** and remove the **G!** And then the **I!** And the two **C's!** What do you see? Nothing!

The **Generator** creates the **Variability** by **Generating the Change-ability.** Without the **Generator,** there is only the increasingly **Restricted Variability** of **The Unfree.** Ultimately, there is only **Totalitarianism!**

With **Generativity,** there is **Change!** The deck gets reshuffled and marginal peoples get new opportunities. Perhaps that is why everyone else is afraid!

In transition, things change! Some people do, too! By way of illustration in 1989, the senior author had occasion to teach at various universities and centers in Rome where he delivered to priests both his presentation and his book on **"The Age of the New Capitalism."** In so doing, he gave instructions for the Vatican priests to hand-deliver the work to Pope John Paul and his staff. Eighteen months later, the Pope issued an Encyclical on **"The New Capitalism."**

Alone among the leaders of the world, Pope John Paul II has addressed vigorously the issues of **Freedom Versus Totalitarianism** in his **Centesimus Annus.** He concluded that the wealth of nations is not so much *"in the ground,"* and therefore deserving of equitable distri-bution (translate socialism), as in the **"Human Mind"** that is infinite in its potential:

> Can it perhaps be said that, after the failure of Commu-nism, capitalism is the victorious social system, and that capitalism should be the goal of countries now making efforts to rebuild their economy and society?... If by

"capitalism" is meant an economic system that recognizes the fundamental and positive role of business, the market, private property and the resulting responsibility for the means of production, as well as free human creativity in the economic sector, then the answer is certainly in the affirmative, even though it would perhaps be more appropriate to speak of a *"business economy," "market economy,"* or simply *"free economy"* (John Paul II, **Centesimus Annus,** 42.1–42.2, in Miller, **Encyclicals**).

The Pope's remaining questions for the future were simply what kind of **"Free Economy,"** based upon what kind of understanding of the **"Acting Person** (Weigel, p. 615)."

What impresses us most is the Pope's changing perspectives. After two millennia of the Catholic Church's belief in **Totalitarian Socialism** as the source of the redistribution of assumedly finite resources, he now promotes both God's greatest creation, **Human Brainpower,** as the source of **Infinite Possibilities,** and **The Free Enterprise System** as the vehicle for its delivery.

The marginal high performing cultures that have been both recipients and influencers of **The Freedom Functions** are numerous. The cultural Jews of 20th century America have demonstrated leadership — culturally, economically, governmentally — by being incorporated by the moving and growing **Freedom Systems.**

Beginning as outcasts of **Totalitarian Societies,** they have become the leading contributors to **Cultural Relating.** Indeed, Jewish leadership among the Freudians and the Neo-Freudians generated the first **Human Relations** systems in the world. To this day, they continue to have leadership roles in the **Helping** and **Human Relations** professions.

Disenfranchised by the "Pogroms" of the **Control Economies** of the East, the Jewish leaders gained financial skills in surviving among varied quarreling economies. They brought these skills to America to be incorporated by the **Free Enterprise** system. Some are now working initiatively to expand **The Old Capitalism** to incorporate **The New Capital Development** ingredients of generating wealth.

Eliminated by the **"genocidal holocaust"** of the German tyranny, the Jews brought their own idealized version of participative governance from the **Weimar Republic** to **"The Great Democracy of the West."** In so doing, they became leaders in the **Civil Rights** and now the **Human Rights** movements. What better way for a once-marginal, now-leading culture to protect the future contribution of all high-performing, marginal peoples?!

Altogether, the Jews of America have been significantly over-represented on *all* indices of constructive functioning—social, scientific, artistic and the same **Per Capita GDP** with which we measure the **Prosperity** of nations. Moreover, they are significantly under-represented on *all* indices of dysfunctionality—psychopathology, criminality, welfare dependency.

In a very real sense, as exemplars for marginality transformed into originality, the American Jews have been both the product and the model for **The American Experience.** Historically, they were the products of **The Freedom Functions.** Existentially, they model them: **Collaborative Relating, Capitalistic Enterprise, Representative Governance.** Futuristically, they may serve among agents for elevating **The American Performance** to actualize **The Freedom Functions: Interdependent Relating, Entrepreneurial-driven Free Enterprise, Direct Democratic Governance.**

To say that there is no national model for the highest levels of **Global Freedom,** however, is not heuristic. America was, to be sure, the model and facilitator for the **Global Marketplace** with its 20th century version of conditions.

However, for a variety of reasons, including the current **World War III,** the U.S.A. has been detoured from its **Collaborative Global Vision** and regressed again to an independent mission.

- America's private sector has produced **"Corporate Terrorists"** who are much more devastating in retarding civilization than any isolated primitive cultural tribes could ever be.

- America's public sector has produced **"Governance Terrorists"** who—in the name of **Freedom**—would strip us of **The Freedom Functions** that we need to grow.

- America's educational sector has produced **"Standards Terrorists"** who—in the name of empowerment—would accelerate the degree of our retardation back to the primitive conditioned responding that they know best and for which we have the least use.

All of this in the land of opportunity that once defined **Freedom** by its creative initiatives!

Today, America comes up short on the very standards that it helped to create:

- **It has become increasingly Independent in its Cultural Relating.**

- **It has become increasingly Mixed between Capitalism and Command Economics.**

- **It has become increasingly Mixed between Representative and Authoritarian Governance.**

To be sure, some crises—not of its own making—have caused America to drift from the standards it established, even as these standards continue to define the requirements for **Global Freedom.**

The once-marginal Jews say it best with their vision of *"Tikúnalam"*— **the betterment of the world through the betterment of the person:**

- **Interdependent Cultural Relating,**
- **Entrepreneurially-driven, Free Enterprise Economics,**
- **Direct Democratic Governance.**

VI. SUMMARY AND TRANSITION

11. The Possibilities Economy

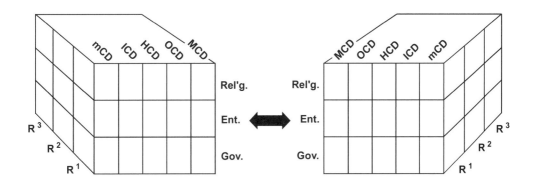

A recent illustration of entrepreneurially-driven free enterprise was demonstrated by **M.I.T.** *According to* **Bank Boston,** *approximately 4,000 entrepreneurial companies were created by M.I.T. alumni and faculty. By 1997, these organizations had generated nearly $250 billion annual sales while creating over one million new jobs. This qualifies the* **"Educational-Entrepreneurial"** *source,* **M.I.T.,** *as one of the leading economies in the world.*

Relatedly, when the senior author conducted a study of the differential characteristics of the **Fortune 500** *and the* **INC. 500** *corporations, he found the following (See Table 3):*

- *While the* **Fortune 500** *companies grew at a yearly average compounded rate of 4% and a five-year growth rate of 17%, the fastest-growing* **INC. 500** *companies grew at a yearly average compounded rate of 82% for a total economic growth of 992% during the same growth period.*

- *During that five-year period, the total employment growth, while negative for the* **Fortune 500** *firms, was over 400% for the* **INC. 500** *companies.*

Table 3. Impact of Entrepreneurial Companies Upon U.S. Economy*

	INC. 500	FORTUNE 500
Yearly Average Compounded Growth Rate	82%	4%
Total Economic Growth	992%	17%
Total Employment Growth	402%	−11%

---

* R. R. Carkhuff. *Human Processing and Human Productivity.* Amherst, MA: HRD Press, 1986.

> *While not all **Fortune** and **INC.** companies generate these averages, the implications are clear. Entrepreneurial businesses are prepotent in generating both economic and employment growth as well as technological breakthroughs.*

"When we choose, we choose for all humankind!" Nowhere is this more true than in the choices that people make for future generations.

When people choose leaders who represent their interests in **Freedom,** they enjoy **Prosperity** and its correlates—**Peace** and **Participation.** At high levels of **The Freedom Functions,** they are blessed with the ingredients of **The Possibilities Economy.**

When people choose leaders who do not represent any interests in **Freedom** or, conversely, when **Totalitarianism** asserts itself, then they do not enjoy the benefits of **Prosperity** and its correlates. At low levels of **The Freedom Functions,** they are dominated by the ingredients of **The Probabilities Economy.**

We can view again the levels of **The Freedom Functions** and their relationships with **Prosperity** in **The Freedom Figure** (See Figure 40):

- The *"losers"* adopt **Totalitarianism** and hover near the bottom of **Prosperity** indices.

- The *"confusers"* see the benefits of **Prosperity** but hesitate to commit to **Freedom.**

- The *"winners"* make increasingly powerful commitments to **Freedom** and receive exponentially greater benefits in **Prosperity.**

"When we choose, we choose for all humankind!"

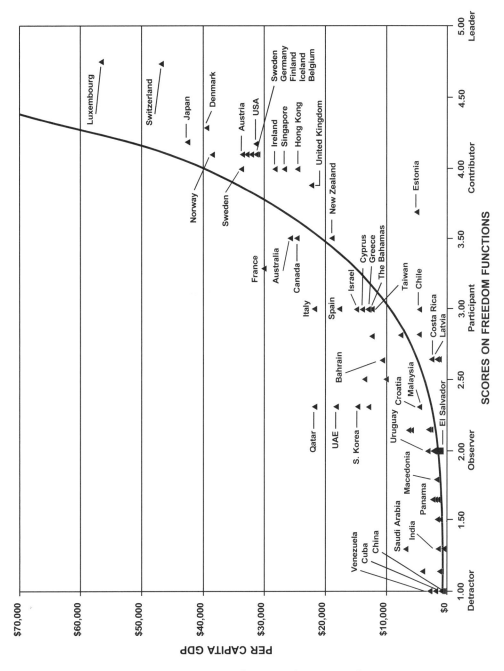

Figure 40. Freedom and Prosperity

Unfortunately, **Totalitarian People** are not always satisfied with the illusion of stasis and security. They seek to prevent other people from achieving the benefits of **Freedom** and **Prosperity.** There are two basic models of humankind and a huge range of people in between these extremes:

- Those who live the basic principle of **Freedom,** *"Do not be less than you can be!"*

- Those who live by the basic principle of **Totalitarianism,** *"No one deserves more than I and mine!"*

Then there are those who hover and judge without committing.

The former are **"winners"** and they struggle to actualize themselves and their families and their cultures and their nations.

The latter are **"losers"** because they struggle, not only to avoid the responsibilities of actualizing themselves, but also to assume responsibilities for attacking those who do.

"When we choose, we choose for all humankind!"

The Possibilities Economy

Like **The Possibilities Science** that yields it and undergirds it, **The Possibilities Economy** is a processing journey (See Figure 41). It is not simply *about* **The Freedom Functions,** nor **The New Capital Development Components** that achieve them, nor the **Generative or Possibilities Processes** that enable or empower them.

It is *living* **The Freedom Functions:**

- **The Free and Interdependent Cultural Relating,**
- **The Free and Interdependent Enterprise,**
- **The Free and Interdependent Governance.**

It is *being* **The Freedom Functions!**

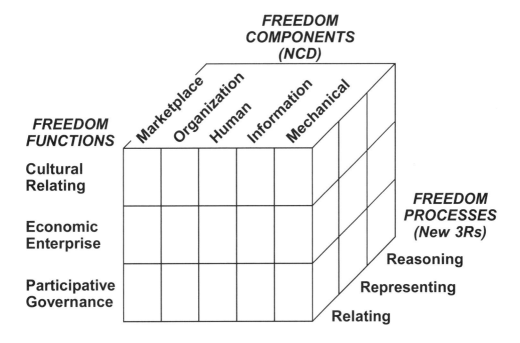

Figure 41. The Freedom Model

Cooperative vs. Collaborative Relating

Collaborative Cultural Relating is *not* about cooperative relating. The latter is defined only as a *"temporary cessation in hostilities"* of otherwise independent and competitive societies. Collaborative relating is a merged initiative between independent parties. It does not mean that we have to *"know"* the culture of our friends or, for that matter, our enemies. It means simply that we can relate to share images and negotiate newly merged images that are of mutual benefit to the values and requirements of all entities.

In the final analysis, relating is about processing or thinking. All relating involves the sharing of images. Indeed, it is the very sharing of images that elevates individual thinking to interpersonal or collaborative processing. To be sure, it is the very unequality of the processing potential of processors that generates the highest levels of relating.

At the highest levels, collaborative relating culminates in **Inter-dependent Processing.** This interdependency is defined as *"mutual processing for mutual benefit."* It is similar to a good marriage where partners are, alternately, unequal contributors: where, for example, one might be a *"delivery system"* in one area and provide a *"support system"* in another area. That is because one knows more or has had more experience than the other. It is because we will deliver the best babies or produce the best products when we set our egos aside to process interdependently.

Multinationals vs. Entrepreneurial Enterprise

Free Enterprise Economics is not about building **Multinational Corporate Giants.** The problem with the **Multinationals** is that, while they are often built upon **Freedom Functions,** they are disposed to abandoning them in favor of *"controlling the market."* This disposition to **"Stasis"** is retarding for the entrepreneurial initiatives of others as well as attenuating for their own corporate existences. In short, while the corporations may follow **The Freedom Functions** to grow, when they abandon them, they begin to look more like the losers: dependent and reactive relating, command-and-control economics, totalitarian governance.

At the highest levels, **Free Enterprise Economics** is entrepreneurially-driven. The entrepreneurs not only produce most of the technological breakthroughs but also the greatest economic growth. Moreover, they are the sources of *all* new employment. At the same time, the vast majority of those who go out of business do so because of shortages in cash-flow and not because of a lack of profitability. In short, we must not only nourish these fledgling operations, but also protect them from the predatory behaviors of the **Multinationals.** Corporate leaders such as Bill Gates of Microsoft send out thousands of scientists and engineers to discover *"the two guys in the garage"* that he fears will create a new market imbalance that cannot be controlled. Of course, *"the two guys"* will receive offers that, one way or another, they cannot refuse and at least their entrepreneurial initiative will be sentenced to death.

Perhaps this is the greatest down-side of **Multinationals:** having achieved market dominance through substance, they seek only market control through **Totalitarianism.** To sum, the **Multinationals** are *"wild-cards"* in the **Market:** they have little allegiance to **The Freedom Systems** that enabled their **Prosperity** — no **Social Conscience! Multinationals** are not the model! They are the danger!

In contrast, the entrepreneurs do, indeed, owe their fidelity to **The Freedom Functions:** without them, the entrepreneurs would not be in existence. **The Entrepreneurial Vision** is consistent with **The Possibilities Vision:** a vision of continuous change in market conditions stimulated by generative scientific and technological breakthroughs empowered by elevated organizational positioning and educational standards for the future.

All of this is not to say that *all* **Multinationals** are tyrannical. There are some that are socially conscious of the root systems that nourished them to become the blossoming flowers they are.

Nor is it to say that all entrepreneurial organizations are "Local-nationals," e.g., bound to their local and national territories. In the **Global Marketplace,** entrepreneurial organizations must also become **"extended enterprises"** in order to flourish and grow.

In the final analysis, capitalism, itself, is a theory of change. It evolves to emphasize the **"most important"** or **"capital"** ingredients in the equation for generating wealth. These new ingredients now emphasize **New Capital Development:** marketplace, organization, human, information, mechanical ingredients. Moreover, the capitalistic system has **"morphed"** into an entrepreneurial-driven, **Free Enterprise** system available to all people everywhere.

Representative vs. Participative Governance

Viewing **Representative Governance** as the highest level of **Participative Governance** is inherently dysfunctional. First of all, in this time of increasing complexity, the representatives do not know how to *"represent"* the various images of information that their constituencies hold: they were never taught to do so and so they distort the images in sentences, systems, scales, schematics and spatial representations.

Secondly, the representatives are unable to process empathically and accurately to develop merged images of the information: **getting** the images of others; **giving** their own images; **merging** new and more productive images.

Thirdly, for many purposes, it is not in the representative's interest to *"represent"* someone else's images. Most representatives' interests are in being re-elected and becoming wealthy. The representatives are supported by the contributions of large, *"status quo"* organizations such as the **Multinationals,** so *"they do not bite the hands that feed them."*

Finally, the representatives, themselves, constitute obstacles to the communication of real constituency needs. Often, they are engaged in decision-making *about* someone else's needs. Most often, the people affected by these decisions do not participate in the process.

At the highest levels, **all persons being affected by** as well as those **affecting** must **participate directly** in the governance process. Ultimately, this will involve some kind of an electronic process. Transitionally, it will emphasize some kind of *"town meeting of the air."* Increasingly, this will require an **enlightened citizenry,** if not products of their schooling — **by any means necessary!**

In the final analysis, democracy is about **"demos"** or **"people"** in Greek: it is about involving people in acting to generate their own destinies. **"Democracy"** and **"representation"** are *not* interchangeable terms. The Republic is a developmental stage in democracy. At the highest levels of democracy, **all** peoples participate in **all** governance.

Possibilities Development

All of the stages of all of **The Freedom Functions** are developmental and cumulative. This means that the lower levels of accomplishment become platforms for higher level achievement. At the highest levels, the dimensions are free, interdependent and initiative. At the lowest levels, the dimensions are unfree, dependent and lacking initiative.

For example, in terms of **Cultural Relating,** we cannot begin to think with real initiative until we relate with true responsiveness. Working with **"Ethnic Think Tanks,"** Dr. Griffin empowers people in empathic understanding by teaching them **"to walk in another's shoes."** Substantively and spiritually, Griffin skills the different cultures **"to find God in the other person."** The **"Ethnic Think Tanks"** merged to initiate legislation to insure that *all* cultures are represented in the initial strategizing phases of legislation impacting *any* of the culture's welfare.

Similarly, in terms of **Free Enterprise,** we cannot begin to initiate entrepreneurially until we have explored experientially. Working with **"New Careers"** candidates, the senior authors empowered unemployed people in entry-level jobs. At the same time, they taught **Possibilities Thinking Skills** that enabled the people to go on to develop all kinds of entrepreneurial and intrapreneurial initiatives in both the private and the public sectors. From a population of functionally-illiterate, seventh-grade educated people, more than 50% went on to achieve college degrees, many went on to create their own businesses, and some became millionaires.

Likewise, in terms of **Participative Governance,** we cannot begin to initiate democratically until we have been empowered substantively. Working with minority and majority community people in a **"Real People's Congress,"** the senior authors empowered the people to converge upon a common initiative: that the disenfranchised peoples should be empowered to represent themselves **"at all points and places affecting their lives—womb to tomb."** The minorities were enfranchised and went on to assume leadership roles in the public sector (one becoming a State Senator chairing the **House Ways and Means Committee**) and the private sector (one sitting on a **Fortune 500 Board of Directors**).

As in most areas of human endeavor, our assets become potential deficits. If we do not continue to aspire to the highest levels of **The Freedom Functions,** then our achievements may become our obstacles:

- **Consensus-built Collaboration** may prevent truly generative **Interdependent Processing** with its conforming mentalities.

- **Capitalistic-driven Multinationals** may neutralize truly entrepreneurial **Free Enterprise** with their **Totalitarian** obstructions.

- **Representative-driven Governance** may short-circuit truly **Participative Governance** with their bureaucratic "distancing."

Indeed, for some who are successful, these scales may be curvilinear: when they get to the **Contributor Level,** they regress to lower levels. Like the **Multinationals** that model this behavior, typically, they regress from **Collaborative, Capitalistic** and **Representative** to **Competitive, Commanding** and **Authoritarian.** Like children, we become mature in order to regress to immaturity.

The net of all this is the following: if we do not continue to process to search out the evolutions of **Freedom,** then we will suffer the retrogressions to earlier stages of conditioning and, indeed, civilization. In short, we can get to the **Contributor Level** by relating interpersonally and functioning mechanically. We cannot get to the **Leadership Level** without processing interdependently and functioning initiatively.

On a humorous note, in presenting success stories of community, cultural and national resource development, the senior author was confronted with the following question: **"Does it work for privileged people, too?"**

We would hate to think that **The Freedom Functions** would discriminate against the privileged the way the lack thereof has discriminated against the disenfranchised! **The Freedom Functions** are skills. As such, they are:

- **Operational,**
- **Learnable,**
- **Achievable.**

We believe that **The Freedom Functions** work for everyone. They are ingredients that made America the world leader in demonstrating multicultural excellence in relating, enterprise, and governance. We also believe that the functions are continuously evolving and elevating and eclipsing previous standards. When practiced skillfully, these ingredients will empower and release nations and their peoples to generate their own **Possibilities Vision.**

The Possibilities Civilization

The Possibilities Vision of **The Freedom Functions** views the highest levels of **The Freedom Functions** to be interdependent, entrepreneurial and direct:

- **Interdependent cultural relating** defined by **"mutual processing for mutual benefit;"**

- **Free enterprise economics** driven by **"mutual trading for mutual benefit;"**

- **Participative governance** defined by direct relating for **"mutual benefit."**

Here, then, is how the highest levels of **The Freedom Functions** interrelate in this vision.

The Possibilities Vision culminates in entrepreneurial initiatives that are defined by *all* areas of **New Capital Development.** Because of the nature of entrepreneurial initiative, not only can anyone share in governance but, indeed, all are asked to generate and share new images.

To be sure, the organizational systems are multidimensional with continuously-rotating functions requiring the realignment of resources. Here there is no **"succession planning:"** only **"succession processing"** in the form of **"continuous interdependent processing."** The latest and best processor gets the most important jobs!

In this context, **The Possibilities Civilization** is an extension of **The Possibilities Economy**—and profoundly so (See Figure 42)! The effects of **The Freedom Functions, The NCD Components** and **The Possibilities Processes** are multiplied exponentially.

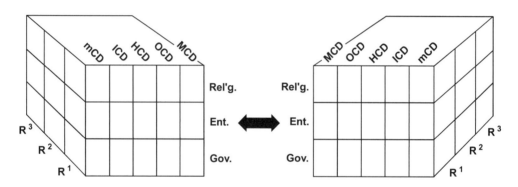

Figure 42. The Possibilities Civilization

Civilization is *living inside* of **The Freedom Functions!**

- The atoms of empathic understanding that constitute the sources of **Cultural Relating!**

- The protons of initiative that comprise the sources of **Free Enterprise!**

- The electrons of attitudes that contribute to the bodies of laws that provide the foundation for **Participative Governance.**

Living inside **The Freedom Functions** means doing so inclusively, vibrantly and with integrity:

- So that interdependent relating is continuous and enduring and, above all else, honest!

- So that entrepreneurial initiative is growthful and culminating and, above all else, substantive!

- So that democratic participation is diverse and, in phases, unequal and, above all else, inspiring!

In transition, the problems with which we wrestle on a daily basis are really products of our own ignorance. For example:

- If we wish to have **Generative Leadership** in the marketplace, we can expand our **R & D** capacities.

- If we wish to have **Innovative Initiatives** to the marketplace, we can elevate our support for **Entrepreneurially-Driven Free Enterprise**.

- If we wish to have **Generative Commercializers,** we can accelerate our **Educational Processing Systems**.

- We can interrelate these initiatives in **Continuous Interdependent Processing "GIC" Relationships:** where **Generator, Innovator** and **Commercializer each contribute synergistically to the other's growth.**

We have just defined major operations of **The Possibilities Economy** and **The Possibilities Civilization.**

There is no longer any need for us to accelerate our degree of retardation.

Above all else, no one need ever succumb to **"Fear of Freedom!"**

At its core, *living inside* of **The Freedom Functions** *is* the substance of **The Possibilities Civilization.** Our divergent phenomenal perceptions make us larger and greater than our individual uniquenesses and serve our convergent missions of intentionality. Our generative processing systems enable us to become guides to our generous and changeable human destinies!

Here are **Ten Principles of a Preamble to the Possibilities Civilization** in which both **Freedom** and **Prosperity** seek to express themselves in continuously-escalating terms.

Preamble to The Possibilities Civilization

The Possibilities Civilization exists in the brains of people everywhere:

- *Where all people count because their brainpower may possess means to both goals and problem solving;*

- *Where all people relate because it is their interdependency and, most of all, the marginality of their perspectives that generates new images;*

- *Where all people empower each other and, especially, the next generations to prepare them with the means to escalating dreams;*

- *Where all people reach for freedom and, in so doing, release all others to do likewise;*

- *Where a spiraling infinity of tailored products, services and solutions services all of humankind;*

- *Where human technologies serve to drive mechanical and information technologies to achieve all things of capital value;*

- *Where human technologies are viewed in the conditions of marketplace, cultural, community and organizational development technologies;*

- *Where the environment and nature are viewed as synergistic processing partners with the growth of each required for the success of all;*

- *Where processing is a necessity and work is a privilege and jobs merely by-products of burgeoning abundance;*

- *Where the resources for which wars are fought are synthetically produced through the generativity of people and the blessings of God;*

"When we choose, we choose for all humankind!"

AFTERWORD

The Possibilities Vision

Hernan Oyarzabal, D.Sci.
Former Executive Director,
International Monetary Fund

There are events of such power that they fill the pages in the evolution of ideas and, thus, the advancement of civilization. Each powerful idea eclipses those that have gone before. **"The Freedom Wars"** is such an idea! Indeed, this great body of work incorporates many such ideas. Let us summarize these ideas in their own operational terms — functions, components, processes, conditions, standards.

The Freedom Functions

First, this work defines the ingredients of the eternal wars between the forces of **Freedom** and those of **Totalitarianism;** moreover, it defines them in operational terms as levels of **The Freedom Functions.** These levels are arranged developmentally and cumulatively from our behaviors in primitive, **"hominid-like"** states to our behaviors in advanced stages of **"humankind"** and civilization. This operationalization means that people and nations can proceed developmentally to accomplish the highest levels of **The Freedom Functions:** cultural relating, economic enterprise, participative governance. Until now, many have conceptualized — but none have operationalized **The Freedom Functions.**

NCD Components

Second, this work defines the components that empower us to achieve **The Freedom Functions.** Historically, we had only the **Financial Capital**-driven systems of the Capitalists and the Resource-distribution systems of the Socialists. Now we have the productivity systems of **New Capital Development** or **NCD:** marketplace, organization, human, information, mechanical. These **NCD Components** address 85% of the variability in **Economic Productivity Growth.** In other words, if we want to grow economically, we must be empowered in **NCD.** Until now, most have viewed economic growth in terms of **Financial Capital.** Now we have operationalized growth in terms of

The New Capital Development calculated to achieve **The Freedom Functions.**

Generative Processes

Third, this work defines the processes that enable **The NCD Components** to accomplish **The Freedom Functions.** Historically, we had only **S–R Conditioned Responding Systems** for accomplishing human endeavors. Today, we continue to revere these memorization systems in our formalized **Standards-of-Learning** and incorporate conditioning in our **S–O–R Discriminative Learning Systems.** Now we have the **Generative Processes** or **Possibilities Thinking Systems** to empower us to create new and more productive responses. These **Possibilities Thinking Systems** enable us to generate entirely new responses that the stimuli were not calculated to elicit. In this manner, we are continually elevating the contributions of **NCD Components** to accomplishing **Freedom Functions.** Until now, then, we have operationalized processing in terms of conditioned responding and, only rarely, discriminative learning. Now we have operationalized processing in terms of the generative processing, especially the individual and organizational processing that make **New Capital Development** possible.

Market Conditions

Fourth, this work defines the conditions of **The Global Marketplace** within which **The Freedom Functions** have their impact. Essentially, the **Global Marketplace** is defined by nations relating for trade. In different instances, some of the nations are rated high on **The Freedom Functions** while others are rated low as, for example, in the **NAFTA** and **CAFTA** treaties between America and its South and Central American trading partners. This differential in functioning is not an obstacle to free trade but, rather, as the authors teach, potentially, a stimulus to generative marketplace processing between otherwise unequal partners. Until now, then, we have operationalized the marketplace in terms of reciprocal trade agreements. Now we can operationalize **The Global Marketplace** in terms of requirements for elevating levels of **The Freedom Functions** and therefore **Prosperity.**

Performance Standards

Fifth, this work defines the standards of **Prosperity** in terms of **Per Capita GDP.** This means that we judge a nation by how it frees its people—culturally, economically, governmentally. Moreover, it means that we judge a nation by how it rewards its people financially. In this context, **Freedom** indices are process measures while **Prosperity** is an outcome index. This extensive work indicates a direct and powerful relationship between **Freedom** and **Prosperity.** Until now, then, we have defined the standards of the marketplace in verbal and conceptual arguments about capitalism and socialism. Now we can define the standards operationally in terms of **Freedom.** All **Free Nations** are **Prosperous!** No **Unfree Nations** are **Prosperous!**

Processing Systems

The greatest differentiator between **Free** and **Unfree Nations** is processing. All **Free Nations** are driven by processing systems. The nations process to position in the marketplace! The corporations process to align with positioning! The people process to initiate entrepreneurially and intrapreneurially! All **Unfree Nations** are driven by conditioning systems. The leader asserts it! The organizations conform! The people adapt! The greatest differentiator between **Free** and **Unfree Peoples,** then, is the processing that generates initiatives. Never before have there been comprehensive **Possibilities Processing Systems** that enable all people to elevate their **New Capital** to accomplish their desired levels of **Freedom Functions.** Even for the high-rated nations such as America there are higher aspirations for **Freedom:** interdependent cultural relating; entrepreneurially-driven, free enterprise; direct democratic governance.

For what is freedom if not generating initiatives for an evolving and escalating experience of **Participation, Peace** and **Prosperity?!**

So it is in the realm of ideas! Once generated, forever generative!

The ideas put forward in this great work will provide a foundation for the great civilizations of the future.

We need no longer conduct **"The Freedom Wars!"** We need only construct progressively escalating civilizations based upon an **"epiphany"** of progressively escalating ideation.

We owe an enduring celebration of gratitude to these authors for their lasting contributions to future generations.

APPENDICES

A. References

References

Berenson, B. G. and Carkhuff, R. R. *The Possibilities Mind.* Amherst, MA: HRD Press, 2001.

Carkhuff, R. R. *Helping and Human Relations, Volumes I & II.* NY: Holt, Rinehart and Winston, 1969.

Carkhuff, R. R. *The Development of Human Resources.* NY: Holt, Rinehart and Winston, 1971.

Carkhuff, R. R. *Sources of Human Productivity.* Amherst, MA: HRD Press, 1983.

Carkhuff, R. R. *The Exemplar.* Amherst, MA: HRD Press, 1984.

Carkhuff, R. R. *Toward Actualizing Human Potential.* Amherst, MA: HRD Press, 1981.

Carkhuff, R. R. *Human Processing and Human Productivity.* Amherst, MA: HRD Press, 1986.

Carkhuff, R. R. *The Age of the New Capitalism.* Amherst, MA: HRD Press, 1988.

Carkhuff, R. R. *Empowering.* Amherst, MA: HRD Press, 1989.

Carkhuff, R. R. *Human Possibilities.* Amherst, MA: HRD Press, 2000.

Carkhuff, R. R. and Benoit, D. *NCD—A Primer for New Capital Development.* Amherst, MA: HRD Press, 2004.

Carkhuff, R. R. and Benoit, D. *The New 3Rs of Thinking: Possibilities Thinking and Individual Freedom.* Amherst, MA: HRD Press, 2004.

Carkhuff, R. R. and Berenson, B. G. *The New Science of Possibilities. Volume I. The Processing Science.* Amherst, MA: HRD Press, 2000.

Carkhuff, R. R. and Berenson, B. G. *The New Science of Possibilities. Volume II. The Processing Technologies.* Amherst, MA: HRD Press, 2000.

Carkhuff, R. R. and Berenson, B. G. *The Possibilities Organization.* Amherst, MA: HRD Press, 2000.

Carkhuff, R. R. and Berenson, B. G. *The Possibilities Leader.* Amherst, MA: HRD Press, 2000.

Carkhuff, R. R., Berenson, B. G., et al. *The Freedom Doctrine.* Amherst, MA: HRD Press, 2003.

Carkhuff, R. R., Berenson, B. G., et al. *Freedom-Building.* Amherst, MA: HRD Press, 2003.

Carkhuff, R. R., Berenson, B. G., et al. *The Possibilities Economy.* Amherst, MA: HRD Press, 2004.

Carkhuff, R. R., Berenson, B. G., and Griffin, A. H. *The Possibilities Culture.* Amherst, MA: HRD Press, 2002.

Carkhuff, R. R., Carkhuff, C. J., and Cohen, B. *IP⁵D — Integrated Process Development: The Possibilities Business in the Possibilities Economy.* Amherst, MA: HRD Press, 2002.

Carkhuff, R. R., Carkhuff, C. J., and Kelly, J. T. *The GICCA Curve: The Possibilities Marketplace.* Amherst, MA: HRD Press, 2002.

Carkhuff, R. R., Griffin, A. H., and Berenson, B. G. *The Possibilities Community.* Amherst, MA: HRD Press, 2002.

B. Primary and Secondary Sources

Primary and Secondary Sources

African Development Bank, *ADB Statistics Pocketbook 2003.* Available at *http://www.afdb.org/knowledge/publications/pdf/statistics_pocket_book2003.pdf.*

Asian Development Bank, *Key Indicators of Developing Asian and Pacific Countries 2002, Vol. XXXIII.* Available at *http://www.adb.org/Documents/Books/Key_Indicators/2002/default.asp.*

Country statistical agencies, central banks, and ministries of finance, economy, and trade. Available at *http://www.un.org/Depts/unsd/gs_natstat.htm, http://www.census.gov/main/www/stat_int.html, http://www.centralbanking.co.uk/links/mof.htm, http://www.bis.org/cbanks.htm,* and *http://www.dir.yahoo.com/Government/Statistics.*

Economist Intelligence Unit Limited. *Country Profile.* London, U.K.: 2002 and 2003.

Economist Intelligence Unit Limited. *EIU Country Report:* London, U.K.: 1996 to 2003.

Economist Intelligence Unit Limited. *Country Commerce.* London, U.K.: 2002 and 2003.

Ernst & Young International Ltd. *The Global Executive.* New York, N.Y.: 2003.

Ernst & Young International Ltd. *Worldwide Corporate Tax Guide.* New York, N.Y.: 2003.

European Bank for Reconstruction and Development, *Country Strategies.* 2002 and 2003. Available at *http://www.ebrd.org/about/strategy/index.htm.*

John Paul II. *Centesimus Annus:* Papal Encyclical, 1991.

Inter-American Development Bank. Available at *http://www.iadb.org*.

International Monetary Fund. ***Annual Report on Exchange Arrangements and Exchange Restrictions 2002.*** Washington, D.C.: 2002.

International Monetary Fund. ***Government Finance Statistics Yearbook, Vol. XXVI (2002).*** Washington, D.C.: 2002.

International Monetary Fund. ***International Financial Statistics, Vol. LV (2002).*** Washington, D.C.: June 2003.

International Monetary Fund. ***International Financial Statistics Online.*** Washington, D.C.: 2003. Available by subscription at *http://ifs.apdi.net/imf/logon.aspx*.

International Monetary Fund. ***Selected Issues and Statistical Appendix, Various Countries.*** Washington, D.C.: 2001 to 2003.

International Monetary Fund. ***World Economic Outlook: Growth and Institutions.*** Washington, D.C.: April 2003. Available at *http://www.imf.org/external/pubs/ft/weo/2003/01/index.htm*.

International Monetary Fund. ***Country Information.*** Available at *http://www.imf.org/external/country/index.htm*.

Miles, M. A., Feulner, E. J., and O'Grady, M. A. ***2004 Index of Economic Freedom.*** Washington, D.C.: The Heritage Foundation, 2004.

O'Driscoll, G. P., Feulner, E. J. and O'Grady, M. A. ***2003 Index of Economic Freedom.*** Washington, D.C.: The Heritage Foundation, 2003.

Organisation for Economic Co-operation and Development. ***OECD Economic Outlook* No. 73,** June, 2003.

Organisation for Economic Co-operation and Development. OECD on-line. Available at *http://www.oecd.org/statsportal/o,2639,en_2825_293564_1_1_1_1_1,00.html*.

Standard & Poor's, *Sovereigns Ratings Analysis.* New York, N.Y.: 2003. Available at *http://www2.standardandpoors,com/NASApp/cs/ContentServer?pagename=sp/Page/FixedIncomeBrowsePg&r=1&1=EN&b=2&s=17&f=3.*

Transparency International, *The Corruption Perceptions Index,* **2002, 2001, 2000, and 1999.** Berlin, Germany: 2002, 2001, 2000, and 1999. Available at *http://www.transparency.org/cpi/index.html#cpi.*

United States Department of State. *Country Reports on Human Rights Practices for 2002.* Bureau of Democracy, Human Rights, and Labor. March 2003. Available on U.S. Department of State Internet site, at *http://www.state.gov/g/drl/rls/hrrpt/2002/index.htm.*

United States Departments of State and Commerce. *Country Commercial Guides.* Washington, D.C.: 2002 and 2003. Available at *http://www.buyusainfo.net/adsearch.cfm?search_type=int&loadnav=no.*

United States Trade Representative, Office of the, *2003 National Trade Estimate Report on Foreign Trade Barriers.* Washington, D.C.: U.S. Government Printing Office, 2003. Available at *http://www.ustr.gov/reports/nte/2003/index.htm.*

World Bank. *World Bank World Development Indicators on CD-ROM 2003.* Washington, D.C.: 2003.

World Bank. *World Development Indicators 2003.* Available by subscription at *http://publications.worldbank.org/WDI/.*

Weigel, G. *Witness to Hope.* NY: Cliff Street Books, 2001.

World Economic Forum. *The Global Competitiveness Report 2002–2003.* Oxford University Press, 2003.

World Trade Organization. *Trade Policy Reviews,* **1995 to 2003.** Available at *http://www.wto.org/english/tratop_e/tpr_e/tpr_e.htm.*

Yergin, D. and Stanislaw, J. *Commanding Heights: The Battle for the World Economy.* New York: Simon and Schuster, 2002.